ORAL LITERATURE, GENDER, AND PRECEDENCE IN EAST TIMOR

ALSO BY DAVID HICKS

Rhetoric and the Decolonization and Recolonization of East Timor

Tetum Ghosts and Kin: Fertility and Gender in East Timor

Kinship and Religion in Eastern Indonesia

A Maternal Religion: The Role of Women in Tetum Myth and Ritual

Structural Analysis in Anthropology: Case Studies from Indonesia and Brazil

Cultural Anthropology (co-author, Margaret A. Gwynne)

Ritual and Belief: Readings in the Anthropology of Religion (editor).

Translator

Peoples of Timor, People of Timor: Life, Alliance, Death by Henri and Maria-Olímpia Campagnolo. Portuguese original, Povos de Timor, Povo de Timor: vida, aliança, mort.

Oral Literature, Gender, and Precedence in East Timor

Metaphysics in Narrative

DAVID HICKS

∴ niasPRESS

Oral Literature, Gender, and Precedence in East Timor
Metaphysics in Narrative
David Hicks

Nordic Institute of Asian Studies
Monograph series, no. 147

First published in 2020 by NIAS Press
NIAS – Nordic Institute of Asian Studies
Øster Farimagsgade 5, 1353 Copenhagen K, Denmark
Tel: +45 3532 9503 • Fax: +45 3532 9549
E-mail: books@nias.ku.dk • Online: www.niaspress.dk

A CIP catalogue record for this book is available from the British Library

ISBN: 978-87-7694-275-5 (hbk)
ISBN: 978-87-7694-276-2 (pbk)

Typeset in Arno Pro 11.5/14.2
Typesetting by Don Wagner
Printed and bound in the United Kingdom by Printforce

Cover illustration: Lake We Lenas, in Fatuberliu Administrative Post,
Municipality of Manufahi (photo Maxine Hicks).

To my darling little grand-daughter,

Clara Juliet,

as promised

Contents

TABLES AND ILLUSTRATIONS

Maps

Plates

Table

Preface

While the majority of the essays about East Timor or Timor-Leste (I employ both alternative designations in this book) that form the substance of this volume have been published as separate studies over the past several decades, they coalesce into certain ideas, themes, attitudes and institutions[1] that in their different ways are given expressive form through the medium of oral literature by the imaginations of generations of East Timorese. Each is concerned, in one way or another, with symbolic revelations primarily in the form of narrative but also as material artefacts, such as the sacred house and a fishing hook, and in cultural themes like gender and precedence that define the Timorese way of life. Nurtured in local culture – or 'cultures' – they also give outsiders (*malai*) glimpses into imaginary worlds and imaginary domains. Chapters 1, 2 and 3 are original, though some of the material that they contain has been published earlier. The essays in Chapters 4–8 remain in much the same form as they were originally published and since they deal with common themes, their contents, at times, overlap. Their sequence follows the order in which they were first published and in some places they reveal a development in my thinking and conclusions. Occasionally, therefore, some repetition is unavoidable, especially as concerns the ritual performed at Bemalai, and certain narratives. Among them are the story of the lazy brother (Chapters 5, 6, and 8) and a narrative I gathered in Caraubalo *suku* (a group of villages *povoações* or *aldeia* administered nowadays in East Timor by a *chefe de suku*) in 1966–1967 that I transcribe in its entirety in Chapter 8 and summarize in Chapter 6. The ritual in question is discussed in Chapters 5 and 8.

---

1   In this book I use the term 'institution' in the sense adopted by Marcel Mauss, that is, as 'public rules of action and thought' (Mauss 1968: 25).

Collecting previously published work together into a single volume suggests a certain degree of conceit on the author's part but I would like to think that these chapters, scattered about as contributions to various journals and edited anthologies, might have value for scholars interested in Timor-Leste, comparative literature, religion, the structural analytical approach to the study of collective thought, and the ethnography of insular Southeast Asia in general. It is gratifying to observe that their traditional oral literature is now exciting enthusiastic attention among East Timorese themselves. In 2016, two scholars, Vicente Paulino and Keu Apoema, published a volume entitled *Tradições Orais de Timor-Leste* that calls attention to the perspectives of indigenous scholars on their own oral traditions while several educated Timorese, Tiago Sarmento prominent among them, use *Facebook* and other websites to display – for the benefit of fellow Timorese – the richness of their wonderful oral traditions. At an earlier time, books by Father Artur Basílio de Sá in 1961, and Ezequiel Enes Pascoal in 1967, introduced dozens of Timorese oral narratives into the published literature. What still remains desirable is to introduce Timorese verbal art into current social-science scholarship by subjecting it to a rigorous scholarly analysis. As individual pieces, these essays contribute, I hope, in some small measure towards attaining this goal and by consolidating them in a single volume my intention is here to take a further step towards achieving a more sustained understanding of Timorese culture than single essays can do scattered throughout the published literature. The fascination that Paulino, Apoema, Sarmento, Josh Trindade, and other Timorese scholars are currently displaying for oral forms of literary expression demonstrates that it is not simply the rural population for whom oral tradition continues to have significance. Their engagement with this art form shows that local narratives cannot be dismissed as mere folktales that simply entertain or instruct. Their engagement with Timorese oral literature lends weight to my argument that this form of indigenous art is capable of revealing philosophical notions about essential aspects of human existence of such sophistication as to merit being considered purveyors of metaphysical insights.

Acknowledgements

I thank the following organizations for their help in funding my research at various times in Timor-Leste since 1966: the London Committee of the London-Cornell Project for East and South East Asian Studies which was supported jointly by the Carnegie Corporation of New York and the Nuffield Foundation; the Frederick Soddy Trust; and the American Philosophical Society; the Harry Frank Guggenheim Foundation; and Stony Brook University. Permission was granted by the Portuguese Government to enable me to carry out my first period of field research in Portuguese Timor. On a more personal note my thanks go to Mr Rui Cinatti, Dr Barbara Ward, Professor Rodney Needham, Professor Fürer-Haimendorf; Father Jorge Barros Duarte; Professor Gregory Forth; Mrs Maria Rosa Biddlecombe (née Maria Rosa da Costa Soares), Mr José Henriques Pereira, Mrs Rosa Maria Pereira, Mr David Soares, Ms Agostinha Soares; Mrs Teresa da Luz Simões Soares; Mr Luís da Costa Soares; Mr Fernando da Costa Soares; Mr José Caetano Guterres; Mr José Texeira; Mr Geoffrey Etches; Ms Marion Corbett; Mr Benjamim de Araújo e Corte-Real; Mrs Lurdes Bessa; Mr Kym Miller, Mr Dan Groshong, and Mr Max Stahl. Assistance regarding certain essays in this volume I also acknowledge in the essay itself.

My greatest debt is to the Timorese people themselves who over decades have provide me with the material for my writings. I hope that they gain some benefit from reading what an anthropologist has to say about their splendid cultures.

I also thank and acknowledge the following organizations and editors for republishing in full or using some material from the following essays: 'Making the King Divine: A Case Study in Ritual Regicide From Timor' originally appeared in *The Journal of the Royal Anthropological Institute (N. S.)* 2: 611–24. 1996. 'Divine Kings and Younger Brothers on Timor' originally appeared in *Structuralism's*

Transformations: Order and Revisions in Indonesian and Malaysian Societies, edited by Lorraine V. Aragon and Susan Russell. Tempe, Arizona: Arizona State University. 1998. 'Younger Brother and Fishing Hook on Timor: reassessing Mauss on hierarchy and divinity' originally appeared in *The Journal of the Royal Anthropological Institute 13 (N. S.)* 13 (1): 39–56. 2007. 'Impaling Spirit: Three Categories of Ontology in Eastern Indonesia' originally appeared in *Animism in Southeast Asia,* edited by Kaj Århem and Guido Sprenger, pp. 257–76. Routledge: Taylor & Francis Group. London and New York: 2016. 'Exchange, Water, and Motif in an Etic Genre of Narrative' originally appeared in *Transformations in Independent Timor-Leste: Dynamics of Social and Cultural Cohabitations,* edited by Susana de Matos Viegas and Rui Graça Feijó, pp. 156–72. Routledge: London and New York. 2017. Some material in Chapter 2 and Chapter 3 appeared in 'Afterword: Glimpses of Alternatives: the *uma lulik* of East Timor' in *'Against Belief?' Social Analysis* 52 (1): 166–80, Special Issue, edited by Simon Coleman and Galina Lindquist, London. Berghanan Books (2008); 'The Barlaque of Timor-Leste' in *Transition, Society and Politics in Timor-Leste,* edited by Paulo Castro Seixas, Porto: Universidade Fernando Pessoa, pp. 115–22, (2010); and 'Compatibility, Resilience and Adaptation: the *barlaque* of Timor-Leste' in *Local-Global: Identity, Security, Community,* Volume 11. Special Edition, edited by Damian Grenfell, pp. 124–37 (2012).

I would also like to thank NIAS Press, especially editor in chief Gerald Jackson for guiding me from the time I submitted my manuscript for publishing; senior editor Leena Höskuldsson for her excellent editing of my manuscript; and Adela Brianso Junquera for spreading the word about this book.

Glossary of Selected Tetum Words

adat	custom
ahi matan	clan, hearth, eye, source
aiknananoik	myths, folktales, fables, morality tales, just-so stories
alin	younger sibling
alin-feto	younger sister
alin-mane	younger brother
barlaki	see *barlaque*
barlaque	term regularly (though incorrectly) used to designate indigenous marriages
bi'in	elder sister
belak	pectoral disk of silver or gold that men wear
berlaki	see *barlaki* and *barlaque*
concelho	under the Portuguese colonial administration one of the 13 districts into which the colony of Portuguese Timor was divided
dato lulik	priest
ema	person, people
ema Dili	people, principally residents of the capital, whose values are aligned with those of educated Timorese and *malai*
ema foho	people of the uplands or interior, the term overlaps with *ema lisan*

ema lisan	persons who follow their *lisan*
fetosa	wife-takers
fetosa-umane	asymmetric alliance
kaibowki (or caibowki)	metal headpiece shaped in the form of buffalo horns worn by men and women
klamar	elemental, soul
lia na'in	a teller of tales, bard, human repository of his or her local community's *lisan*, today term also used to include an officer of the local government
lia(n) tuan	legends
lisan	'tradition', custom
lulik	sacred, set apart, forbidden
makair lulik	see *dato lulik*
malai	foreigners, outsiders
matan do'ok	shaman, curer
mate bein	ancestor (*mate* = death, dead; *bein* = ancestor)
mate klamar	soul of a recently deceased person
morteen	necklace of coral beads worn by women
Posto Sede	under the Portuguese colonial administration the seat of local administration for a district (*concelho*)
rai inan	earth mother
rai laran	the spiritual world (see also *rai seluk*)
rai na'in	lords of the earth, a term denoting both earth spirits and human autochthous owners of a tract of land
rai seluk	the spiritual world (see also *rai laran*)
sasan lulik	sacred family heirlooms passed down from generation to generation
suku	a group of hamlets, village

Tetum Dili	a form of Tetum with many foreign words, spoken widely in East Timor, a national language (as 'Tetum')
Tetum Terik	that form of Tetum indigenous to certain Timorese populations
Timor oan	a native of Timor-Leste
uma cain	household; extended family; nuclear family
uma laran	see *uma cain*
uma lulik (also uma lisan)	ritual house
uma lisan	see *uma lulik*
umane	wife-givers in the *fetosa-umane* institution
we (or u'e)	liquid, water, source, point of origin
we na'in	lords of the water, water spirits

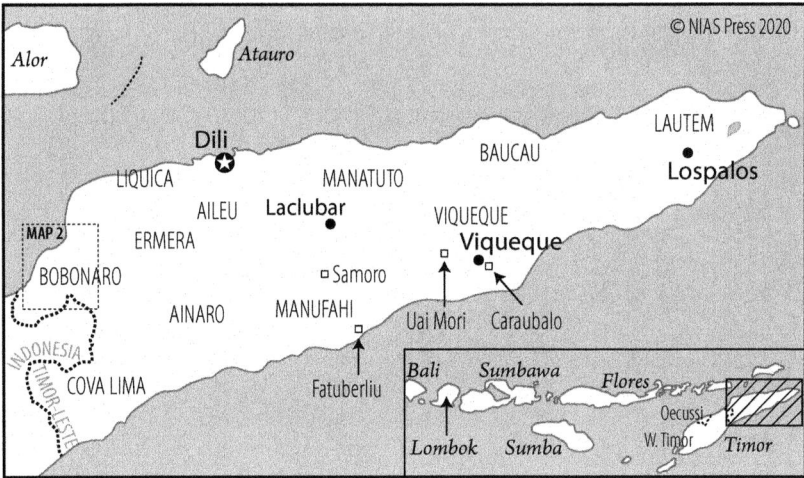

Map 1 East Timor

David Soares talking to the author in 2005

CHAPTER 1

Introduction

C urrent interest among East Timorese (or *Timor oan*) in their
own culture by is by no means limited to oral and written
literature. We find it attested to in material form. This is
evident from the extensive construction that has been going on since
independence of an artefact that embodies the traditional culture of
East Timor – the aforementioned sacred house or *uma lisan* (or *uma
lulik*). This building stands – quite literally – as a material embodiment
of the customs (or customary laws) or *lisan* (or *adat*) of its people at
the same time as suggesting, for Josh Trindade at least, a potentially
unifying symbol of Timor-Leste's future as a nation-state. As a material agent attesting to the continuing presence of the ancestors or *mate
bein* (*mate* = death, dead; *bein* = ancestor) in the lives of their human
kin, sacred houses are scattered around the Timorese landscape,
expressing, in the most tangible of ways, the material embodiment of
matter and spirit conjoined, a recurring motif in narrative.

Marriage, typically identified (though problematically, as I shall argue) as the *barlaque*, is as prominent a Timorese institution as the *uma
lisan* is a conspicuous cultural icon and it makes habitual appearances in
fictional plots. These may occur in metaphysically-charged tales, as when
a younger brother (*alin-mane* or *alin*) encounters underwater spirits, or
in more prosaic stories like our first tale that explains how a certain *suku*[1]
acquired the name 'Wai Mori' and how the king of Viqueque gained
precedence over of the ruler of an adjacent territory called 'Fatu Lia'.

---

1   A *suku* is a group of villages (*povoações* or *aldeia*) administered nowadays
in East Timor by a *chefe de suku* whose office in some *suku* coincides with
the traditional office of *liurai*, a political figure usually referred to in the
literature as a 'king'. Whether they occupy the office of *chefe de suku* or not,
liurai can play an influential role in *suku* governance, and should they have
as councillors the *lia na'in* ('lords of the word), the latter can play quite an
influential role in local politics.

1

The notion of precedence is epitomized in the institutional relationship between younger brother and elder brother whose importance in the social order may explain why so many ontologically-themed narratives use it in plot devices that bring about the convergence of the two domains of human and spirit.

Most Timorese ethno-linguistic groups share a common Austronesian heritage and their respective cultures reflect this commonality, as we shall see in the narratives transcribed in the chapters that follow, a heritage that extends, of course, over vast stretches of the Pacific, South East Asia, and includes the island of Madagascar. Accordingly, certain of the stories come from outside Timor.

Current interest in oral literary forms is not confined to East Timorese narratives as the recent publication of *Savu: History and Oral Tradition on an Island of Indonesia* by Geneviève Duggan and Hans Hägerdal demonstrates while, further afield, oral and written forms of literature have garnered popularity, as the publications of A. H. Johns, a scholar of Malay oral tales and court chronicles and those of the anthropologist Susan Rodgers, would indicate. Rodgers has incorporated into the genre of indigenous narrative autobiographical genre from Sumatra and although literature in its oral mode has occupied a central place in the cultures of Timor for centuries its recognition as a literary storehouse of cultural wealth is today not only being enriched by the work of Timorese scholars, it is also being complemented by an exciting new development in Timorese literature that directs its fictions from orality to an emergent written form located in the novel. Its exponent is Luís Cardoso, author of *Crónica de uma Travessia a Época do Ai-Dik-Funan*, which appeared in 1997, and five other novels.[2]

While drawing upon typologies of indigenous genres in literary texts gathered among non-literate peoples, Western scholars tend to favour their own conventional categories and apply such labels as 'myths', 'legends', 'folktales' and 'fables' to the alien texts that they

2 A well-thought-out case study on how orality adapts to the introduction of literacy into a culture is Susan Rodgers' study of Angkola Batak (Rodgers 1984).

study. Sometimes the indigenous culture provides little assistance in this task, for a culture may lack specific terms to distinguish among its various forms of narratives. In East Timor, speakers of the dominant language Tetum, like those of other Timorese languages, classify oral narrative into several categories. *Lia tuan* (*lia* = 'word', 'language', 'speech', 'term', 'to speak'; *tuan* = 'ancient', 'venerable', 'worthy of respect', 'important') are tales that contain at least one event, circumstance, or character that is empirically impossible and/ or describes the origins of significant features of the natural environment and the origins of humankind and accordingly fall into J. van Baal's definition of 'myth' (Baal 1977: 165) or legend. The Tetum category, *aiknananoik*, includes stories describing human adventures, animal rivalries, and the origin of place names. It embraces fables and other genres of narrative, and might be considered 'folktales'. Father Artur Basílio de Sá, a Catholic missionary and authority on Tetum language and oral tradition (Sá 1961: 8), derives the etymology of the term *aiknananoik* from *aik* = 'tree', wood and *nananoik* = 'narrative, story, tale', from the custom of orators reciting their tales under the spreading branches of a large tree, though in Viqueque I found that orators prefer the verandas of houses as the location for recitations.

As with the story of Monkey in Narrative 1 (Chapter 2), *aiknananoik* may serve a pedagogic function, even if only implicit, as well as entertainment and in this respect, as well as in its lack of concern with genesis and freedom from corporate ownership by descent groups, this particular *aiknananoik* contrasts with the majority of the narratives in this book. These tales that feature Monkey as a protagonist generate much amusement among listeners who, as I can bear witness, delight in hearing how Monkey's agile brain enables him more often than not to overcome a more physically impressive rival (sometimes Dog, sometimes Crocodile, sometimes Shark), though not, as it happens, in Narrative 1.

In their painstaking and ground-breaking analysis of *lulik*, Bovensiepen and Rosa (2016) quote a Portuguese colonial officer who described 'the indigenous imagination' of the Timorese as lacking the capability to 'sketch out metaphysics'. One purpose of the essays collected together in this volume is to refute this claim by arguing that, although on first appearance the narratives transcribed in them may seem to be simple accounts about the doings of younger brothers, elder brothers, denizens of the deep, crocodiles, snakes, and birds, and infuse mundane objects like fishing hooks with an importance out of all proportion to the modest place that they occupy in ordinary daily life, they can, when regarded from the perspective of structural analysis be revealed as tales that engage with ontological matters and harbour themes of metaphysical significance. Another is to contest Catholic missionaries' view that Timorese 'confuse matter and spirit' (Bovensiepen and Rosa 2016: 677). I attempt to demonstrate that, to the contrary, Timorese thinking – as revealed in these narratives – most decidedly recognizes matter and spirit as distinct categories.

REFERENCES

Baal, J. van 1977. Review of *Le symbolism en général* by Dan Sperber. *Bijdragen tot de Taal-en Volkenkunde* 133: 163–65.

Bovensiepen, Judith and Frederico Delgado Rosa 2016. 'Transformations of the Sacred in East Timor'. *Comparative Studies in Society and History* 58 (3): 664–93.

Cardoso, Luís 1997. *Crónica de uma Travessia: A Época do Ai-Dik-Funan.* Alfragide, Portugal: Publicações Dom Quixote.

Mauss, Marcel 1968. *Oeuvres: 1. Les fonctions sociales du sacré.* V. Karady (ed.) Paris: Les éditions de Minuit.

Paulino, Vicente and Keu Apoema 2016. *Tradições Orais de Timor-Leste.* Dili: Universidade Nacional Timor Lorosa'e (UNTIL).

Rodgers, Susan 1984. 'Orality, Literacy, and Batak Concepts of Marriage Alliance'. *Journal of Anthropological Research* 40 (3): 433–50.

CHAPTER 2

The *Ema Lisan*

T his chapter is intended to establish the socio-cultural setting for the narratives that follow, tales that draw their motifs, in the form of plots, characters, and incidents, from the society and culture that inspired them.

The *ema lisan*[1] are the people of the *lisan*, i.e., they are the people who follow the *lisan*, whose observance is typically justified by reference to 'the words of the ancestors'. The term *lisan* itself refers to customary practices and is the Tetum language counterpart of the Malay term *adat*. It embraces the institutions, values and ideas of what might be characterized as Timorese 'tradition', a word, however, that requires a cautionary note since 350 years of Portuguese colonialism and even lengthier contacts with populations from outside of Timor have resulted in a synthesis of cultural attributes that were not necessarily created or endorsed by the ancestors or transmitted in oral narratives or verse.

Accordingly, Timorese 'traditional' values cannot simply be assumed to provide an unvarnished reflection of the past and when we examine what local communities believe to have been created by their ancestors in ages set in some remote, mythological era we more often than not find that they originated outside Timor-Leste. This is hardly surprising since Europeans have been a presence on the island since the 16th century and Chinese and others in earlier centuries. That political figure known as the *liurai*, for instance, who might otherwise qualify as an exemplary instance of a traditional political category, upon examination turns out to be a synthetic compound of indigenous culture, Portuguese influence, and legal mandates from today's

---

1   The designation *ema lisan* overlaps with *ema foho*, the 'people of the uplands or interior'. Both designations are customarily contrasted with 'ema Dili', i.e., those people, principally residents of the capital, whose values are more aligned with those of educated Timorese and *malai*.

central government. The same process of syncretism may be observed in the case of another figure prominent in 'traditional' Timorese society, the *lia na'in*, whose role as a 'teller of tales', or bard, and human repository of his or her local community's *lisan* has been expanded by government directive into an officer of the local government.

One must also exercise caution in referring to 'Timorese society' or 'Timorese culture', since local *lisans* reflect diverse physical habitats and histories. As these vary across the island, so too do their respective *lisan*. Each *suku* has its own *lisan* which is distinctive and unique to it, though in most respects neighboring *sukus* often have many institutions in common, especially if they speak the same language.

Another term whose connotations overlap to some extent with those of *ema lisan* is *ema foho*, 'people of the uplands' or 'dwellers of the interior', and is generally used to contrast local cultures with that of town-dwellers, pre-eminently those who reside in the capital Dili, the *ema Dili*.

LANGUAGES

Until recently travelling around East Timor was both arduous and protracted, a fact of Timorese life that facilitated the evolution of many different languages and diverse *lisans*. More linguistic research is needed before it can be established exactly how many languages can be identified in East Timor but they number at least fifteen and several languages display significant dialectal variations in vocabulary and phonology.

The languages spoken on the island can be classified into two broad groups, Austronesian and Non-Austronesian. The Austronesian languages are Tetum, Mambai, Meto (or Atoni), Ema (or Kemak), Kairui, Waimaha, Galoli, Nauete, Tokode, and Idaté. On the island of Atauro,[2] Rêssuk, Raklung'u, and Rahêssuk are spoken (Duarte 1984: 11). In Indonesian Timor Meto has the largest number of speakers, followed by Tetum, with a much smaller language group called Helong. Among the non-Austronesian languages in East Timor are Makassai, Fataluku, and Bunak.

---

2   Atauro is an island located about 30 kilometres off the north coast of East Timor opposite Dili.

6

The dialect of Tetum spoken in those regions of East Timor where it is the indigenous language is called *Tetum Terik* in contrast to the dialect of Tetum that is now the national language and spoken throughout the country. This is variously referred to as *Tetum Praça, Tetum Maka,* or *Tetum Dili* and includes a large number of loan words from Portuguese, Indonesian, and English.

Since Tetum is the national language and is spoken by the majority of Timorese – in one dialectal form or another – the vernacular terms used in this book come (except where noted otherwise) from Tetum.

NARRATIVES

Timorese oral narratives entertain, provide support for *lisan,* instruct, and explain how topographical features of local landscapes, human beings, descent groups (clans and lineages), and social and political inequalities originated. A common theme often involves a stranger who enters a foreign land, marries the local chief's daughter, and settles down as the senior man's political subordinate.

The narratives in this book come from various ethno-linguistic groups, and their plots, characters, physical setting, and institutions express the daily experiences of those who recite and listen to them. And since Timor is an island subject to months of aridity it is not perhaps surprising that references to water (both salt and fresh) occur time and time again in many of these stories. It typically functions as the medium facilitating passage between the world of matter and the world of the spirit by a representative of one or other of these domains, with a lost fishing hook or some such implement as the material agent enabling the conjunction. Once in the other world the representatives of both domains enter into a relationship which is often mutually beneficial. Such tales depend upon a staple of social life – the unequal relationship between the elder brother and the younger brother, who loses his sibling's hook in the water.

Other constituents of *foho* life are the cultivation of maize, rice, vegetables, and root crops, complemented by the raising of buffaloes, pigs, goats and chickens. These facets of quotidian existence impart a certain realism to the fictitious worlds the tales portray, as do the appearance of animals like dogs and monkeys which are a ubiquitous presence and whose human counterparts are those key figures in daily life, the elder brother and the younger brother. *Lisan* prescribes that the two brothers co-operate and tales in which Dog and Monkey appear provide listeners with an allegorical lesson in how to behave and how not to behave, as our opening narrative illustrates. Listeners to the narrative learn how Monkey and Dog decline to follow the prescriptions enjoined by *lisan* and instead indulge in behavior antithetical to domestic order. As we shall see their altercation, which involves cooking, food, and drink, breaches *lisan* etiquette and has lethal consequences for both 'elder brother' Dog and 'younger brother' Monkey.

Narrative 1. Monkey and Dog[3]

Monkey bought a goat that he took into the middle of a wood. He started a fire, It blazed up and Monkey began roasting the goat in *tuquir* fashion[4] when along came Dog. His appearance scared Monkey so much he tried to trick Dog. 'Oh. Dog! Go and kill some men and steal their wine', he said. 'Bring it here and we two can share the meat!' Off went Dog. Monkey, too, moved, but he climbed to the top of a tree. Dog returned with some wine, and upon arriving called up to Monkey: 'Come down and bring your meat!' Monkey replied: 'Bring your wine and then we both can eat and drink at the top of this tree.' Dog replied: 'What! But I am so very bad at climbing trees! Just toss me a little meat and I'll eat here on the ground!' But Monkey said: 'You shall eat only the bones, Dog! I'll give you the bones because you are just a dog. Eat them up, and then get back to your garden!' At these words Dog

---

3   This narrative was generously recited for my benefit by João Lopes and Edmundo on the night of 26–27 January 1967, in their village of Mamulak, in Caraubalo *suku*. The former was the principal reciter. The text originally appeared in Hicks (1973a: 93–100).

4   A method of cooking in which minced meat, either by itself or with rice or chopped vegetables, is thrust into a bamboo tube about two feet long before being cooked on hot stones or in hot cinders.

pretended to die. Monkey then believed it was safe to descend the tree, and after he had done so began to kindle a fire in which to roast Dog. Monkey started to take hold of Dog's head to roast it, but was too scared. He next started to take hold of Dog's leg to roast it, but again was too afraid of Dog. Finally, he grabbed Dog's head to roast it, and Dog bit his throat. 'Oh, *maun* Dog, you are biting me!' he exclaimed, 'Speak to me!' But Dog did not want to, and instead continued biting Monkey until Monkey was dead. Dog's owner arrived and tied up Monkey's body, picked up the goat meat and took Dog home. Both Goat and Monkey were eaten.

A recurrent characteristic of 'Monkey' narratives is that Monkey fits into the inferior social role of younger brother while his rival (and erstwhile partner) fits into that of elder brother. This relationship binding agnatic males of the same genealogical level has a substantial jural and ritual significance that is framed within the context of precedence. The elder brother is entitled to deference from his younger brother and in certain domestic situations acts as a surrogate for the father. The relationship of precedence, however, is reversed at the conclusion of narratives of the lost fishing hook.

Of unequal kinship status though they are, the elder brother and younger brother are entangled in a complex system of rights and duties which entail their interdependence and complementarity. The Monkey and Dog narrative transcribed above gives literary expression to this inequality with Monkey being fearful of Dog at the same time as the tale reflects the ideal of cooperative harmony being violated by the anti-social qualities of greed, nastiness, and selfishness. At the same time the plot plays upon the hostility latent in this sibling relationship that finds open expression in the ensuing fight.

KINSHIP, MARRIAGE, AND AFFINITY

For all the ethno-linguistic groups in Timor-Leste, the importance of kinship, marriage, and affinity can scarcely be overestimated. For the *ema lisan* the *lisan* governs how property is inherited, where a just-married husband and wife reside after marriage (i.e., their post-marital residence), and the web of rights and duties that marriage entails for those who provide the wife and those who receive the wife (see Chapter 3). Land ownership and eligibility for political office, such as *chefe de suku* (*suku* chief), traditionally required the candidate to be a member of a specified descent group (*uma*), a corporate social entity that anthropologists conventionally term a 'clan' (Tetum: *ahi matan*: *ahi* = 'fire'; *matan* = 'eye', 'centre', 'source') or one of the smaller groups into which clans are typically divided, *viz.*, a lineage (Tetum: *ahi fuan*, *we fuan*). These lineages consist of extended families (*uma laran* or *uma cain*), the locus of which are nuclear families or households (*uma cain* or *uma laran*).

The majority of *sukus* follow a patrilineal mode of descent. Bride-wealth is given in exchange for the person of the wife; the husband continues to reside patrilocally after marriage; and the offspring of the marriage belong to the husband's descent group. The wife leaves her father's house and takes up residence within her husband's circle of patrilineal kin. The social mechanism making this possible is bridewealth and its implications for gender are of such consequence that foreigners (*malai*) when discussing gender in Timor-Leste have taken a passionate interest in what they take to be its institutional expression, marriage, which they generally refer to – misleadingly, as I shall argue in the next chapter – as 'the *barlaque*' (or '*barlaki*')'[5]. The extensive social, political, economic, and ritual ramifications of this central *lisan* institution is reflected in the frequency with which it appears in narratives that describe bonding between two men. In narratives weighted with metaphysical import this bonding occurs between the ruler of the spirit world (*rai na'in* or *we na'in*) and a younger brother. In more prosaic tales the bonding occurs between a land-owner (*rai na'in*) and a visiting stranger. The former partnership may take the form of the spirit ruler offering the younger brother the gift of a daughter in marriage. In the latter partnership the scenario almost invariably results in the stranger marrying into the land-own-

---

5   Matrilineal descent accompanied by uxorilocal post-marital residence occur in some *sukus* in Manatuto district, among some Tetum-speakers in Viqueque, and in a few localities elsewhere. It does not, of course, entail bridewealth.

er's family and settling down on his land, thereby becoming doubly subordinate as son-in-law and tenant – a genre of narrative pervasive in clan histories where it justifies contemporary claims on land as well as political precedence, and explains how affinal relationships and place-names came about. The following narrative, from the *Posto Sede* of Viqueque, is typical.

Narrative 2. *The Origin of 'Uai Mori'*[6]

A long time ago in the land of Fatu Lia in the kingdom of Venilale there lived three aristocratic rulers who were highly respected by their subjects. One day the youngest of three, a man named Manu-Lai, decided to visit his relative, the king of Viqueque, but did not know where the king's domain was located. He only knew that the territory lay somewhere to the south. This uncertainty led him to select as traveling companions only those men among his warriors in whom he had special confidence and on the appointed day they set off in a southerly direction (*tassi mane*).

Arriving at a place called Bua-Nanaru the men made camp. They cut down some palm-leaves which would dry out by the time the warriors returned that way and be taken home to be made into mats to cover the floors of the men's houses. Because they had stopped and made camp, Manu-Lai began to make a rope for tethering their horses when in the distance he saw a wounded buffalo come towards him pursued by many hunters. As soon as they saw Manu-Lai the hunters called out to him to run because the creature might attack him, but he pretended not to hear and let the buffalo approach. When it came near enough Manu-Lai jumped up, plucked a stem from one of the leaves he had gathered and killed the buffalo. This incredible feat astounded the hunters who asked Manu-Lai his name, what land he came from, and his destination. To these questions he answered: 'I am a Fatu Lia ruler

---

6   Accessed in the files of the Administration, *Posto Sede*, Viqueque, in 1966, as a typescript in Portuguese dictated by the then *suku* chief, António da Costa Rangel, on 18 March 1964. An earlier version of this narrative appeared in Hicks (1974: 124–60).

travelling south to find a relative who is the king of Viqueque.' At these words the hunters immediately dispatched a messenger to let their king know that a ruler from Fatu Lia claiming to be a relative had come to visit him.

Upon receiving the message the king promptly sought the advice of his councillor, the *dato uain*, who advised him to go with a group of subjects to meet his relative. The visitor would have to be [ceremoniously] carried on a *manu-sila* and escorted by warriors. This was done. When Manu-Lai, his companions, and his escort of honour approached, the *dato uain* sent a servant ahead to tell the king. With his family and many others the king went to greet his visitor.

When the Fatu Lia ruler arrived at the king of Viqueque's residence the latter ordered those persons of aristocratic social rank to throw a feast to honour his guest. The feast lasted seven days during which the king, in recognition of the ruler of Fatu Lia's visit, gave his youngest daughter in marriage to him as well as the authority to govern his subjects, though Manu-Lai would remain under the Viqueque king's authority.

When the wedding was over Manu-Lai decided to return to his own land and with this destination in mind he and his bride departed. After many miles' journey the couple arrived at a hill called 'Uai Kuku' where they noticed a stream flowing down its slopes. There they resolved to build their house. They called the locality 'Uai Mori', a name which means 'running water', and this is how the name of the *suku* of Uai Mori originated.

PRECEDENCE IN THE SOCIO-POLITICAL ORDER

Elder Brothers and Younger Brothers

Privileging of the elder brother (*maun*) at the expense of his younger brother (*alin-mane*) is a salient manifestation of a value that shapes relationships involving family, gender, the social hierarchy, and political norms of Timorese culture, viz., social inequality, which Victor T. King (1985: 12–21) defines as 'the process of unequal distribution of and/or unequal command over key resources such as materials, goods, ritual objects, knowledge and skills'. Among the *ema lisan* an individual's social status derives in the first instance from his or her social class. The importance of class has much diminished in recent decades but the concept of three social classes continues.[7] The majority of the population are *ema reino* or 'commoners'. Immediately above is the social class of *dato*, or 'aristocrats', and above that class is the *liurai* or 'royalty' class. In the past marriage between individuals in different social classes, though never prohibited, was frowned upon but today the ranks are permeable and by dint of education, wealth, or profession a person can elevate his or her social standing.

The Ancestors (Mate Bein)

Lisan is said to have been transmitted from generation to generation from the time of the first ancestors who now reside in the spiritual world. This shadowy domain stands in contrast to the human world but is accessible by human beings by ritual and verbally in oral narrative and in the recitation of certain forms of verbal verse. The ancestors share the spirit realm with a variety of other elementals, nature spirits (*rai na'in*) and souls (*klamar*) of maize and rice and buffaloes. *Sukus* in some regions have a belief in a male god in the sky and a female god located in the earth.

Human beings obtain the gift of fertility – essential for successful rice and maize harvests, the reproduction of clans, buffaloes, pigs, and goats – by offering sacrificial gifts to their ancestors. These gifts consist of pork, buffalo meat, chickens, rice, and betel-chew and are carried out in private ceremonies within the household or publicly as when members of descent groups celebrate the rites of passage of birth, marriage, and death.

LULIK

Engrained in the Timorese world-view is a concept known in the Tetum, Nauete, and Mambai languages as *luli* or *lulik*; in Bunak as

---

7   Social classes among the Fataluku are somewhat different.

po; in Fataluku as *tei*; and in Makassai as *falun* (Trindade n.d., p. 1). Standard Tetum dictionaries provide its referents as 'sacred' and 'forbidden' and I follow this abbreviated definition here. However, in the most definitive analysis of the concept that has yet been published, Josh Trindade shows *lulik* to be a considerably more complex idea than the standard gloss would lead one to think. He describes it as having cosmic connotations that depict it as the spiritual moiety in a dual cosmos whose other moiety is the world of empirical experience. '*Lulik*', he remarks, 'refers to the spiritual cosmos that contains the divine creator, the spirits of the ancestors, and the spiritual root of life including sacred rules and regulations that dictate relationships between people and people and nature' (Ibid.).

Trindade aligns his interpretation of the Timorese cosmos with the emphasis on binary oppositions that we find in the structural perspectives of Claude Lévi-Strauss and the ethnographic analyses undertaken by F. A. E. van Wouden rather than with the monist alternatives that currently engage discussions about animism (Ibid.: 4–5). Into this bifurcated cosmic model of spirit, which is sacred (*lulik*), and matter (or material experience) an analogically-ordered plethora of other binary oppositions finds places. They include a contrast between that which is indigenous to Timor and that which is foreign (*malai*) and a contrast between inside and outside. Furthermore, the *lulik* moiety is a female, inside, world [8] and as such in opposite to the secular (*sa'un*), masculine, outside world. The *lulik* moiety is the repository of (passive) authority unlike the secular world which is the repository of (active) power; *lulik* is a domain associated with ritual; the *sa'un* domain is concerned with the practical; *lulik* is also associated with the pig (a species linked more closely with the feminine than masculine) and forms a binary with the buffalo (a species with masculine connotations); [9] spirit is symbolized

---

8 'In Timorese society woman often are referred to as *feto maromak* (women is [sic] sacred)' (Trindade n. d., p. 12).

9 In the reciprocal rights and duties connecting wife-takers and wife-givers in the *fetosa-umane* form of marriage discussed in Chapter 3, the 'female' wife-takers receive pigs from their 'male' wife-givers and reciprocate with buffaloes.

by rice (and food in general) whereas the secular, male, world is symbolized by machetes and guns, and so forth (cf. Ibid.: 6, for explanatory diagrams). The behaviour of human beings in the secular domain is answerable to the authority of *lulik* which punishes transgressions of *lisan*. 'If an individual breaks *Lulik's* rules and regulations, he or she will be punished in this life … the punishment strikes not only the individual transgressor, it can also strike his or her immediate family their clan or whole society' (Ibid.: 16). Both the ancestors and *lulik* enforce *lisan*: 'If *Lulik* is disregarded by the society, ancestral sanctions will strike society in the form of conflict and disaster, be it natural, social or political.' This understanding of *lulik* implies that, unlike conventional interpretations of the concept which focus on the function of *lulik* as a boundary marker that warns humans against approaching that which is 'set apart' or 'forbidden' by taboos, Trindade interprets *lulik* not merely as set of prohibitions externally applied to whatever is considered *lulik* but a vital force inhering in that object – whether ritual houses, trees, springs, streams, rocky outcroppings, mountain peaks, and vents in the ground, ancient Portuguese documents, rattan sticks (*oe*) that symbolize authority, crucifixes, or pectoral plates (*belak*). The ancestors are involved, too (cf. 'Objects and houses are *lulik* when they contain an ancestral presence', Bovensiepen and Rosa 2016: 671).

Besides this metaphysical character, which I infer Trindade attributes to *lulik*, is a moral philosophy which he considers to define and order social relationships of consequence. Trindade (n.d., p. 2) singles out as especially important the reciprocal ties that bind younger brothers with elder brothers and those linking wife-takers (*fetosa*) with wife-givers (*umane*). As with other transgressions of *lisan*, breaches of the mutual obligations involved in these relationships invite retribution by the powers commanded by *lulik*.

Life, health, fertility, and social accord depend upon the cosmos remaining in a state of harmonious balance that due observance of *lisan* and respect for *lulik* maintains. 'The main objective of *Lulik* as a philosophy', writes Trindade, 'is to ensure peace and tranquility for society as a whole, in which it can be achieved through a proper balance between the real world and the cosmic world. In this case,

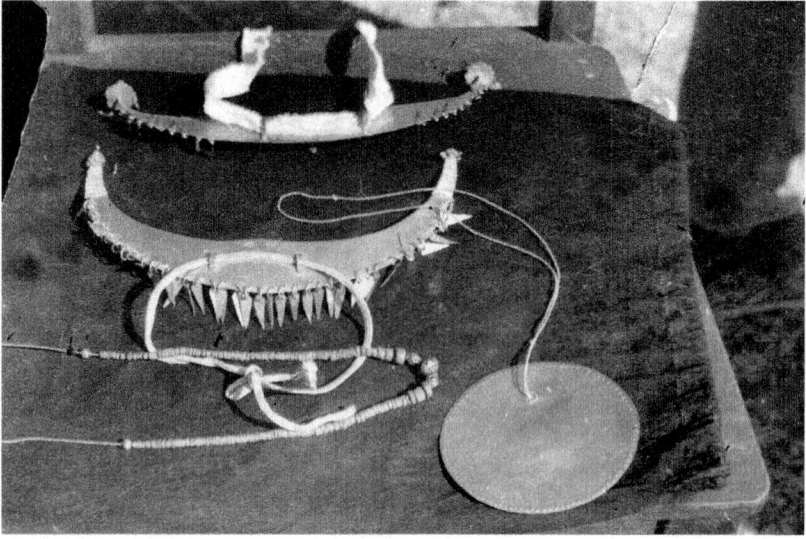

Photo: Maxine Hicks.

Plate 1 Ancestral artefacts: *kaibowki, morteen,* and *belak* (Posto Sede, Viqueque, 1967).

people in the real world should follow the rules and regulations set by the ancestors' (Ibid.).

Additional insights into the nature of *lulik* have come from two other important studies that have notably enriched our understanding of *lulik* by directing our attention to its dynamic nature. Her ethnographic research among the Idate-speaking population living in the central upland community of Funar, in Laclubar, permits Judith Bovensiepen (2014) to confirm the ambivalent character Trindade detects in *lulik* as an agency that provides humanity with benefits at the same time as dealing out punishments to those who transgress its injunctions. Her article calls attention to the danger that arises when human beings physically venture too closely, too carelessly, or with malicious intent into or upon those spaces in the landscape or objects classed as *lulik*[10] and by doing so brilliantly identifies another function of *lulik*: that of safeguarding the human individual's self-identity. Applying Valeri Valerio's and Mary Douglas's ideas concerning taboo to *lulik* and taking into account the humanlike qualities attributed

---

10 Narrative 2 in Chapter 4 and the narrative entitled 'Bemalai' in Chapter 5 illustrate the dangerous potential of *lulik*.

to the ancestral ghosts who, of course, are not human, Bovensiepen argues that too close a proximity between spirits and human beings would erase the distinction between them; thereby endangering the self-identity of the human being doing so. And at the ultimate level, I would argue, erase the metaphysical distinction between two ontological domains and so turn cosmic order into chaos, a process I consider in detail In Hicks (1973b).

Building on the insights of these two essays, Bovensiepen and Rosa (2016) describe how, during the years of Portuguese colonization and Catholic missionary activities, the notion of *lulik* underwent transformation as it incorporated artefacts from the world of the *malai*, as it did, for example, with Catholic crucifixes and statues of the Blessed Virgin and referring to Catholic priests as *nai lulik* (*nai* = 'lord', 'master').[11]

I would argue that these original insights into the nature of *lulik* make it possible to interpret the younger brother's round trip into the underwater realm (which is a central motif in many of the narratives) as a venture by humanity into the spiritual world of *lulik*. On each occasion the younger brother's advance towards and departure from the spirit world is conducted with due respect for the integrity of each ontological realm with a result that is mutually beneficial to both spirit and mortal. The spirit is restored to health or otherwise revitalized while the man gains material wealth, an increase in social standing, or both.

Certain heirlooms (*sasan* [possessions] *lulik*) passed down from generation to generation are classed as *lulik* and as such accorded much deference. They are typically kept in the ritual house, a building heavily imbued with symbolic significance and a Timorese instance of what Victor Turner has called a 'dominant symbol' and Eric Wolf has termed a 'master symbol', which Wolf defines as 'a symbol which seems to enshrine the major hopes and aspirations of an entire society' (Wolf 1958: 34). As such, it is understandable that Trindade and Bryant Castro have proposed the creation of a national *uma lulik* that

---

11 'It may even be that Timorese ancestral ritualists saw the 'presence' of Catholic objects as affirming the spiritual potency and precedence of their indigenous powers' (Bovensiepen and Rosa 2016: 684).

might function as a unifying symbol for the nation-state of Timor-Leste (Trindade and Bryant Castro 2007).

THE *UMA LULIK*

Timorese narrative uses natural space (frequently water) for encounters between spirit and matter but the conjunction can also take place in a cultural setting. One such setting is the *uma lulik*.

Occasionally a ritual house can be found standing in its own parcel of land but more often we find an *uma lulik* located inside a hamlet (*knua*), a house-cluster consisting of nuclear or extended families (*uma laran*). Ritual houses are usually elevated on pillars and accessible by bamboo ladders, but variation occurs. Some have no windows and their interiors – usually a single room bare of furnishings save for one or several woven mats – are dark. They may have a loft and all have hearths (*uma matan*) consisting of a square tray within which rest three round cooking stones. In the roof thatch a few husks from the most recent first harvest of maize and rice are placed and the family heirlooms that I mentioned earlier are affixed to or rest on shelves. They consist of war swords (*surik*), fragments of old Portuguese flags, masculine pectoral disks (*belak*), half-moon head-pieces (*caibowki*), and feminine necklaces (*morteen*), bracelets (*keke*) and cloth (*tais*). Some artefacts have special significance because they play a role in narrative plots that account for how they came into the family's possession. The origins of some of these heirlooms date from the early years of the Portuguese occupation when the affiliation of the owners' ancestors with the Portuguese administration was formally acknowledged in official documents that sometimes bestowed a military title, such as lieutenant-colonel, on the head of the household. The *uma lulik* itself and its contents are in the care of a male or female guardian responsible for safeguarding and maintaining the building and who may live in a building adjacent to the *uma lisan*.

Besides being a place where mortals and ancestral ghosts communicate, the *uma lulik* may also give artefactual expression to the conjunctive complementarity between masculine and feminine in its use of doors, with one door reserved for males and the other for females. Within the house each gender may also be allocated its own space.

This was the case with a Mambai *uma lisan* on the outskirts of Dili I entered in 2005 (Photographs 2 and 3). Inside, the hearth was off-centre to the room and adjacent to the male entrance. Halfway along the room's south side rose a smooth post, roughly six inches in diameter, and at its base was a perpendicular stone perhaps a little over a foot in height and of a dark colour. For my benefit a local person kindly identified the complex of artefacts as a Mambai 'cultural symbol', in which the pillar was the *hun* ('base', 'lower part', 'beginning', 'origins') and the stone was the *fatuk* ('stone'), i.e., 'the *hun ho fatuk*' ('the base and the stone'). At the top, and on either side of the pillar, were attached a small pair of buffalo's horns, a small pair of goat's horns, and several pig jaw bones, *aides-mémoires* of sacrifices offered to the *mate bein*. At the foot of the pillar were a few woven baskets, one with a cover and containing betel leaves, areca nuts, and lime for betel-chewing; the other was empty.

This is the *uma lisan* (or *uma lulik*) in its artefactual sense and these two alternative designations also denote the descent group or household that owns it and whose social identify it materially embodies. It is the prime space where the identity of the living members of the descent group merges with that of its ancestors. Although the building symbolizes the social collectivity of the group owning it, in their attempts at conversion Catholic missionaries disregarded its associations with living human beings and chose instead to perceive the *uma lulik* as an expression of ancestor-worship and an embodiment of indigenous values that they believed impeded their attempts at proselytization. They accordingly encouraged those whom they persuaded to convert to the Christian faith (a small percentage of the population) to destroy them.

As well as ritual houses, shrines and altars to the ancestors and nature spirits that dotted the Timorese landscape as places where Timorese sacrificed to their ancestors or nature spirits (*rai na'in*) became targets for the Catholic missionaries and their presence today bears witness to their latter's failure to convert the population whole-

Photo: Maxine Hicks.

Plate 2 The Mambai *uma lulik* (outside Dili, 2005).

Plate 3 Matter and spirit conjoin: interior view of the
Mambai *uma lulik* (2005).

Photo: Maxine Hicks.

Photo: Maxine Hicks.

Plate 4 Gender conjoined: a male and female Fataluku
uma lulik (Lospalos, 2005).

Plate 5 Hearth in a Fataluku *uma lulik* in Lospalos (2005).

Photo: Maxine Hicks.

Plate 6 A Tetum *uma lulik* in Fatuberliu (2005).

Plate 7 Another view of the Tetum *uma lulik* in Fatuberliu (2005).

Photo: Maxine Hicks.

Plate 8 *Surik*, machete, and baskets inside the Tetum
uma lulik in Fatuberliu (2005).

scale. As late as the early 1970s, out of a total population of 659,102, the number of Timorese who might be counted as Catholics was only 196,570 (Dunn 2003: 40)[12] and just how committed those might have been to Christianity is impossible to estimate. Nevertheless, some of the converts did decide to express their devotion to their newly found faith by dismantling or burning their family's ritual house and even destroying their *sasan lulik*. As well as demonstrating a willingness to sever ties with their ancestors, a family's destruction of its sacred house also threatened to obliterate its self-identity by, in effect, conceding that generations of the family's forebears had been misguided in following the ways of the ancestors. The group's connections with the spirit world identified in *lisan* faced obliteration and the destruction of its ritual house meant that the rituals carried out there would be either abandoned or physically relocated to other – less conspicuous – locations where they would constitute less of a visible affront to the Catholic Church.

Not only did Catholic missionaries look upon ritual houses as a challenge to the authority of the Church, they saw their own role as ritual mediators diminished by the presence of indigenous practitioners *lisan* furnished: priests (*dato lulik* or *makair lulik*), shamans (*matan do'ok*), and the guardians of the sacred houses. Given the contested nature of the *uma lisan*, then, it was hardly surprising that in 1966–1967 people in Caraubalo told me they no longer existed in their *suku*.

Forty years later they proudly showed me the skeleton of an *uma lisan* that they were constructing. Yet even as they were acclaiming 'tradition' the present was acknowledged. Women were busy weaving cloth, preparing food, and collecting the wherewithal for a feast celebrating the ordination of the first local man ever to enter the priesthood. And so far as I could judge no one seemed the least disquieted by what, to a *malai*, would have appeared a contradiction of ideologies.

---

12 There is some discrepancy among the several estimates given for the size of the Catholic population and the syncretic character of Catholicism should also be borne in mind when attempts are made to evaluate the extent to which the missionaries succeeded in converting the Timorese to Catholicism.

The construction of these ritual houses is merely one manifestation of a phenomenon currently occupying villagers all over East Timor and may perhaps be a reaction to their experience during the twenty-four years (1975–1999) of Indonesian occupation when the administration continued the Church's anti-*uma lisan* policy. The Indonesians did so partly because in the administration's view *lisan* failed to satisfy the Indonesian Government's definition of religion but principally because the authorities regarded the ritual houses as manifesting Timorese identity and thus frustrating the Indonesian policy of making Timorese Indonesian citizens.

The coming of Independence, on 20 May 2002, has seen a return to the open display of *lisan* and with it the extravagant rebuilding of its most prominent artefactual expression. Some ritual houses are built or rebuilt to fulfil the ritual needs of households, others to satisfy the more public ritual needs of descent groups. But whatever the social group involved the building once more provides an unthreatened repository for *sasan lulik* and space where ghosts and their human kin are able communicate and proclaim to kin, affines, and neighbours alike their unique history and celebrate a past that distinguishes them from other families. At the same time the *ema lisan* are being obliged to respond to the challenges the Timor-Leste Government and international organizations are forcing on them as well as with the skepticism of modern-minded fellow Timorese. *Ema lisan* understand that a range of alternatives to the values bequeathed them by their ancestors are available. Yet many defiantly reaffirm their identity not only as members of kin groups but as individuals whose identity is shaped by the unseen world where dwell their ancestral ghosts whose words continue to guide them.

Families pay a practical price for expressing devotion to *lisan* in this form since building or even rebuilding a ritual house entails a weighty deployment of human energy and diverts significant economic resources away from productive investment in children's education and health or purchasing consumer goods like refrigerators. Modern-minded Timorese and agency workers are often outspoken critics of this consequence of *lisan* and they have a cogent argument

27

because constructing ritual houses requires not only the labour of a hundred men and women or more for weeks on end but also requires skilled craftsmen and oversight by ritual practitioners to ensure that form and function correspond to ancestral-sanctioned tradition. These can amount to a substantial expense.

As I remarked earlier, Josh Trindade and Bryant Castro have proposed the erection of a national *uma lulik* that could serve as a unifying symbol for Timor-Leste and which might help counter those centrifugal social, political, and economic forces that some observers believe vitiate Timor-Leste's capacity to survive as a nation-state (cf. Hicks 2007a). Their proposal is consistent with Marcel Vellinga's claim that material artefacts can reconstitute a society's values (Vellinga 2007) and if their suggestion were adopted it might result in a greater consolidation of national identity in local communities. Future generations of *Timor oan* may even come to regard national consciousness as a *lisan* value that was transmitted to them by their ancestors.

But as it is, the *uma lulik* is today an iconic institutional expression of *lisan* that continues to be an object that attracts divisive controversy. And not the only one. Generating at least as much criticism, especially from *malai*, is the aforementioned *barlaque* whose consequences in the context of gender inequality will be discussed in the following chapter.

REFERENCES

Berthe, Louis 1961. 'Le mariage par achat et la captation des gendres dans une société semi-feodale: les Buna' de Timor Central'. *L'Homme* 3: 5–31.

Bovensiepen, Judith 2014. '*Lulik*: Taboo, Animism, or Transgressive Sacred? An Exploration of Identity, Morality, and Power in Timor-Leste'. *Oceania* 84: (2): 121–37.

Bovensiepen, Judith and Frederico Delgado Rosa 2016. 'Transformations of the Sacred in East Timor'. *Comparative Studies in Society and History* 58 (3): 664–93.

Campagnolo, Henri 1979. *Fataluku 1: Relations et Choix, Introduction Methodologique a la Description d'une Langue 'non-austronesienne' de Timor Oriental.* Paris: Centre National de la Recherche Scientifique.

Capell, Arthur 1943/1944. 'Peoples and Languages of Timor'. *Oceania* 14–15: 19–48; 191–219; 311–37.

Carmo, António Duarte de Almeida de 1965. *Mambai: contribuição para o estudo do povo do grupo linguístico Mambai – Timor. Estudos Políticos e Sociais (Instituto Superior de Ciências Sociais e Política Ultramarina, Lisboa),* Vol. 3 (4): 1233–1368.

Cunningham, Clark 1972. 'Atoni'. In *Ethnic Groups of Insular Southeast Asia,* Vol. 1: *Indonesia, Andaman Islands, and Madagascar,* Vol. 1. Frank M. Lebar (ed.) Pp. 103–105. New Haven: Human Relations Area Files Press.

Duarte, Jorge Barros 1984. *Timor: Ritos e Mitos Ataúros.* Lisboa: Ministério da Educação (Instituto de Cultura e Língua Portuguesa).

Dunn, James 2003. *East Timor: A Rough Passage to Independence.* New South Wales, Australia: Longueville Books.

Fox, James J. 1971. 'Semantic Parallelism in Rotinese Ritual Language'. *Bijdragen tot de Taal-, Land- en Volkenkunde* 127: 215–55.

Hicks, David 1973a. 'Tetum Narratives: an Indigenous Taxonomy'. *Ethnos* 1–4: 93–100.

—— 1973b. *An Ethnographic Study of a Timorese People.* D. Phil. dissertation, University of Oxford.

—— 1974. 'A Cairui Myth'. *Stony Brook Anthropologist* 1: 124–30.

Sá, Artur Basílio. 1961. *Textos em Teto Literatura Oral Timorense,* Vol. 1. Lisboa, Junta de Investigações do Ultramar, Estudos de Ciências Politicas e Sociais 45.

Trindade, Josh n. d. '*Lulik*: The Core of Timorese Values'. Accessed 13.02.2020. www..academia.edu//7450617/.

Trindade, José and Bryant Castro 2007. 'Rethinking Timorese Identity as a Peace Building Strategy: The Lorosa'e-Loro Monu conflict from a Traditional Perspective.' European Union Technical Assistance to the National Dialogue Process in Timor Leste. Dili: GTZ.

Vellinger, Marcel 2004. *Constituting Unity and Difference: Vernacular Architecture in a Minangkabau Village*. Leiden: KITLV Press.

Wolf, Eric 1958. 'The Virgin of Guadalupe: a Mexican National Symbol'. *Journal of American Folklore* 71 (279): 34–39.

CHAPTER 3

Gender and the *Barlaque*

L ike the construction and rebuilding of ritual houses the
institution known as the *barlaque* (or *berlaki*) attracts critical
attention from *malai* and some educated Timorese. They
offer several reasons for this negative attitude, among them the fact
that the *barlaque* can make excessive economic demands on families
and that it has the potential to force young people to delay marriage.
For many critics, however, the most serious charge is that the *barlaque*
belittles the female gender and in doing so is inconsistent with what
are termed 'international values'. In this chapter I shall argue that the
last accusation is unfounded. Insofar as they involve gender rights,
there is no incompatibility between the values of this ubiquitous institution and international values regarding gender. I shall also argue
that even as outside forces are changing certain of its social, economic,
and political characteristics, the *barlaque* will endure as an integral
part of Timor-Leste's culture.

THE SEMANTICS OF THE *BARLAQUE*

The *barlaque* is an institution misunderstood by many foreign critics.
Some of this misunderstanding results from the confusing semantics
of the word *barlaque* itself, which in addition to denoting bridewealth
can also refer to several distinct, albeit overlapping, forms of marriage
arrangement. Even its etymology encourages confusion since, though
a stock criticism of the *barlaque* is that it involves 'buying a wife', in
its root form – the Malay word *berlaki* – the term glosses as 'to take a
husband'. Further confusion comes about because the term has come
to be invested with religious undertones.

It is not surprising, then, that definitions of the word *barlaque* diverge almost as much as they converge. Father Jorge Duarte (1964:
92–93), quotes the definition of Cândido Figueiredo, 'to buy a

woman according to pagan rituals' and Manuel Patrício Mendes (1935) gives the definition 'marriage among pagans', 'to marry in pagan fashion', and notes that it is 'a word of foreign origin and little used among Timorese'. Artur Basílio de Sá (1961: 151–52) glosses the word as 'a pagan marriage, celebrated by non-Christians'; Luís Costa's dictionary (2000) defines *barlaque* as 'marriage'; a 'matrimonial contract (according to traditional usages and customs) which involves an exchange of goods of equivalent value between the families of the affianced couple'. Geoffrey Hull's dictionary (2002) renders *barlaque* as a 'traditional marriage contract involving the payment of brideprice'. As a scholar and son of a Mambai mother and European father, Duarte is especially qualified to offer a gloss and he confirms Mendes's definition. 'First of all', he remarks, 'it has to be noted that the term *barlaque* is not used by the Timorese except when speaking to *the Malai*, whether a private person or an official' (Duarte 1964: 92)[1] and notes that when used as a substantive, *barlaque* has two referents: 'marriage celebrated between pagans' and the 'prestations' given to the fiancée's parents. In the latter sense, Duarte adds, the term *barlaque* is synonymous with *folin* ('brideprice' or 'bridewealth'[2]). He remarks that 'a great number of Christians, of one or other kind, also celebrate the ceremonies of the *berlaki* in respect of the compensation owing the bride's father, a sort of civil pagan marriage taking place before the religious

---

1 '*Antes de mais nada, tenha-se presente que o termo* barlaque *não é usado pelo timor senão quando fala ao malae, indivíduo particular ou entidade oficial.*'

2 The case for and against employing the terms 'bridewealth' and 'brideprice' were scrupulously adjudicated by E. E. Evans-Pritchard (1931) in the early nineteen-thirties as one of a number of contributions made by social anthropologists on the topic. He concluded that the latter word was too restrictive in its meaning and misleading in its implication, namely that the bride is an object of commerce. He considered that the former, on the other hand, while including the economic implications of the prestations, renders more accurately their wider social and ritual functions. Even so, as he noted, neither English word truly conveys the rich connotations attached to the indigenous terms employed locally in some societies. Timor-Leste is a telling example of this, as we shall see.

marriage. Others, less instructed, remain in the state of pagan marriage, i.e., dispense with the Catholic ceremony. Because of this, in the Portuguese spoken in Timor, *barlaque* and *barlaquerar-se* have come to designate simple marital unions among the indigenous population or among Europeans' (Duarte 1964: 94). According to Duarte, Christians who marry under the auspices of the Church are also permitted by the ecclesiastical authorities to marry according to their local *lisan* which typically would involve giving the *folin*[3], an instance of religious syncretism my wife and I observed in August 2005 in Viqueque town when we were guests at a *liurai* wedding. Both wife-givers and wife-takers were devout Catholics yet the wedding – a very grand and splendid event – included the observance of certain *lisan* ritual embellishments and bridewealth.

My field research confirms Duarte's and Mendes' remarks. During my nineteen months' residence in Viqueque and Baucau I never heard the word *barlaque* uttered and to the best of my knowledge *Tetum Terik* speakers in Viqueque have no generic term that corresponds to the English word 'marriage' but have three categories each denoting a different mode, of marital union[4]: the *fetosa-umane*[5], the *hafoli*, and the *habani*[6] (Hicks 2004: 98–99). The first two categories involve the bridegroom's descent group (whether a clan, a lineage, a sub-lineage, an extended family, or a nuclear family) giving *folin* to the bride's descent group. The *fetosa-umane* is the most elaborate of these modes, generally requiring a *folin* of larger dimension, more demanding in the reciprocal obligations imposed upon affinal partners, and involving

---

3 Clergy, for the most part, continue associating the *barlaque* with *gentio* ('pagan') customs, regardless of whether or not the *folin* is given.

4 These categories are ubiquitous in Timor-Leste.

5 Other terms are used in different languages: in Ema (Kemak), *maneheu-um-amane*; in Bunak, *malu-ai*; in Mambai, *fetosa-umane*; in Meto, *feto-mone*; in Makassai, *umaraha-tupumata*; in Fataluku, *arahopata-tupurmokoru*; in Galoli, *vassau-umane*; in Kairui, *uasa-umane*; in Naueti, *oa-sae-uma ana*; and on the island of Ataúro, *anaperani-anahata*.

6 For a detailed description of these categories of marriage, see Hicks (2004: 94–102).

a network of affinal groups.[7] The *hafoli* is a simpler institution with fewer mutual obligations. A more modest *folin* is given and typically establishes a relationship between only two nuclear families. Both affinal modes, according to *lisan* traditions, though, require that the bride depart her parents' home for that of her husband and that their children belong to their father's clan. In the *fetosa-umane* in particular, wife-givers and wife-takers gather together to celebrate the birth of a child or the death of an affine, public occasions that demonstrate their mutual obligations.

The *habani* lacks the *folin* and the newly-wed husband leaves his father's house to reside with his father-in-law. His children belong to his wife's clan.

The English word 'marriage' may also be applied to other marital or quasi-marital modes of union. In 1966 in Viqueque there existed an arrangement in which no *folin* was given yet the son-in-law did not have to live and to reside with his wife's father, an arrangement called *hafen* (*halo* = 'to make' + *fen* = 'wife'), which was not regarded with much respect. Duarte (1964: 93) mentions its occurrence in Dili (where at the time of his writing was employed as a synonym for *habani*) and in other places where *Tetum Praça* was spoken. He provides as its gloss, 'contracting pagan marriage without the obligation of giving the *folin*; or simply for a woman to enter into a condition of concubinage'. He also identifies among the speakers of *Tetum Terik* a form of marriage called *ha-etu*, in which the husband incurs the obligation of supporting his bride and giving to her parents and relatives a simple pre-nuptial gift of more modest dimensions than the regular *folin*. Duarte considers it scarcely amounting to a bridewealth at all (ibid.). He regards *hafe(n)* as a synonym of *habani*, though he does not mention the husband having to reside with his father-in-law. Another form of marriage in Dili is the *aitukan-be-manas* (Silva 2010: 129–30) that involves a bridewealth of between 500 and 3,000 dol-

---

7   The importance of the *fetosa-umane* is underscored by Trindade who, it will be recalled (Chapter 2), notes that the reciprocal obligations that wife-givers and wife-takers owe to each other in this institution are enforced by the powers of *lulik*.

lars. Some families who engage in this form of marriage say that this is not the *barlaque* because the *aitukan-be-manas* is given only to the wife's biological parents and not to other relatives of the bride's; but Silva discovered two instances that refuted this claim: the *folin* was given to the bride's uncles and cousins. With all these permutations and different terms it is no wonder the *barlaque* confuses most *malai*!

Further complication comes about because in some *suku*s in Manatuto, in certain Tetum-speaking *suku*s in Viqueque district, and among the Bunak on the border with West Timor, matrilineal descent and matrilocal residence occur (cf. Chapter 1). Under this regime of descent and post-marital residence no *folin* is given and the children belong to their mother's line. Does the term *barlaque* apply to this arrangement? Since, according to Duarte, the term *barlaque* can be applied to all forms of non-Christian marriage, this would appear so, but in that case, what comes of the 'buying a wife' argument?

THE *BARLAQUE* AS AN INSTITUTION

One source of misunderstanding can be resolved easily enough. Writers on the *barlaque* are often wont to call it a 'dowry'.[8] Now, *The Oxford English Dictionary* (2000: 1003) defines the word 'dowry' as '[t]he money or property the wife brings her husband; the portion given with the wife'. In *The American Heritage Dictionary* (1992: 558) the dowry is defined as '[m]arriage or property brought by a bride to her husband at marriage'[9]. *Folin*, therefore, is decidedly *not* a dowry. *Folin* is 'brideprice' or 'bridewealth', i.e., prestations given by wife-takers to wife-givers. In general terms, a *folin*'s dimensions reflect the social status of the two affinal groups, the relative wealth of the wife-takers, and local *lisan* protocols.[10] Its magnitude can be so

---

8   See, for example, Sousa (2001: 188).

9   The Oxford dictionary does, it is true, offer the gloss: 'A present or gift given by a man to or for his bride', but it notes this usage as being obsolete.

10 Of the different language groups in Timor-Leste, the Fataluku – so I am informed by Timorese with whom I have discussed the matter – are reputed to require the largest *folin*. On the other hand, I have heard it said that this

disproportionate as to discourage marriage and has the potential to deplete a family's economic resources.

The *fetosa-umane*, we might note, is by no stretch of the imagination a parochial institution exclusive to Timor. In much the same form it is found in other regions of the world[11] where it has received thorough attention from anthropologists who refer to it variously as 'generalized exchange', 'asymmetric alliance', and 'matrilateral cross-cousin marriage'.[12] According to its protocols, men (wife-takers) marry the sisters and daughters of men in other descent groups (wife-givers) and give their own sisters or daughters as wives to the men of another descent groups as part of an established system of marital alliances that may persist from generation to generation. Bridewealth is exchanged for these females and the direction of this exchange of women is strictly unilateral and is not subject to reversal. In other words, wife-givers are not permitted to take women from their wife-takers and wife-takers are not permitted to give women to their wife-givers.

Ideally, a man should marry into a wife-giving group that is already allied with his own, preferably the descent group from which his mother came. Hence the expression '*matrilateral* cross-cousin marriage'. A man's prospective wife therefore would be his genealogical mother's brother's daughter (MBD) or perhaps a classificatory MBD. The ideal for a woman would be to marry a man from among her own descent group's wife-takers. This would include her biological or classificatory father's sister's son (FZS). A man is not permitted to marry his father's sister's daughter (FZD), i.e., his patrilateral cross-cousin, nor a woman marry her mother's brother's son

---

is more in the way of cultural self-regard by persons of that language group rather than what typically happens when most marriages take place.

11 In mainland and maritime Southeast Asia local variations of the Timorese *fetosa-umane* are defining features of the societies in which they occur, as among the Kachin of northern Burma (Leach 1951), the Lamet of Cambodia (Needham 1960), various Batak groups of Sumatra (Rodgers 1984), and the Rindi of eastern Sumba (Forth 1981).

12 This is from a man's perspective.

(MBS), i.e., her matrilineal cross-cousin. In practice, life being what it is, individual marriages may diverge from the ideal and marriage between men and women whose descent groups have no prior affinal ties may be common enough. In such cases new alliances are formed and these extend the range of a descent group's affinal networks, which can result in mutual benefits. In the *Posto Sede* of the Viqueque of 1966 the most egregious violation of the rule would have been for a pair of men to marry each other's sisters, an infraction of the *lisan* thought to incur sanctions from the ancestral ghosts that would probably cause the union to be infertile.

Since a descent group, then, may have multiple wife-giving and wife-taking partners, each of which has multiple wife-givers/wife-takers of its own, one consequence of asymmetric alliance is the creation of an extensive network of affinal relationships, a characteristic that Claude Lévi-Strauss recognized when he described this mode of affinal alliance as 'generalized exchange' (Lévi-Strauss 1949). Nevertheless, although these networks may or can include any number of groups, the system can be reduced to a simple triadic model as F. A. E. van Wouden (1935) and Lévi-Strauss (1949) have demonstrated. Although these cyclical alliances can bind alliance groups for several generations, the greater the number of groups in a particular cycle the more prone the cycle is to breaking up because, for instance, descent groups may be unable, owing to demographic changes, to maintain their alliances and 'fall out' of the network. Brigitte Clamagirand has described how these systems change and reports instances among the Ema (or Kemak) in the region of Marobo where 'a system of marriage alliances according to a four-partner cycle' has evolved into a three-partner cycle (Clamagirand 1980: 111–15).

It might be worth remarking that the existence of asymmetric alliance in Timor has long been known.[13] Dutch administrators and

---

13 The literature on the *barlaque*, though not voluminous, is not insignificant. Besides the works referred to in the text an interested reader would find the following useful: Cunningham (1967) and Hicks (1973; 1978; 1981; 1983; 1986; 1987; 1989; 1990; 2004). And for asymmetric alliance elsewhere, Leach (1951) and Needham (1962) are standard works.

scholars have identified the system in West Timor and among the first writers to mention it in East Timor were the English naturalist, Alfred Russel Wallace (1869), and his fellow countryman, Henry O. Forbes (1884), in the late 19th century. In the 20th century the Portuguese administrator, Armando Pinto Corrêa, gave a preliminary account of the *umarahe-tupumata* among the Makassai in his monograph, *Gentio de Timor* (1935), which is richer in ethnographic detail than either of the two English writers' accounts. More recently Lourenço Marques da Silva has analysed the system in his *Barlake Tuir Lisan Emar Makasae-Soba* (2003) that carries special authority since da Silva is himself a Makassai from Ossu.

Among some ethno-linguistic groups this asymmetry, which as we have seen is a defining feature of generalized exchange, is verbally signalled in the kinship terminology. A man calls his female matrilateral cross-cousin (MBD) by a different kinship term from the term he employs to denote his female patrilateral cross-cousin (FZD). A Naueti man, for example, calls his MBD *bunara* and his FZD *buana* (Hicks 2007: 255). A Naueti woman calls her MBS *kria* and her FZS *kriana* (Hicks 2007: 255). Since the system anticipates, as it were, a man marrying his MBD the term for MB may also denote WF, as among the Nauete where the category (*obu*) includes both relatives.

Whether the groups involved in these alliances are clans, lineages, sub-lineages or families, the relative social status and symbolic attributes of wife-giver differ from those of wife-taker. Wife-givers have precedence over wife-takers and, as already remarked, designated the 'masculine' group. Wife-takers are 'feminine' and subordinate. The prestations given to wife-takers by the wife-givers are 'feminine' prestations. They include cloth, pigs, rice, women's coral necklaces and the most valuable gift of all, the bride herself. The counter prestations, given by the wife-takers, the bridewealth, is classed as 'masculine' and comprises buffaloes, horses, goats, chickens, men's gold or silver pectoral plates, war swords, and money. The bride, it must be emphasized given the controversy about 'gender inequality' in Timor-Leste, is but one component – and by far the most valued – in an extensive and reciprocal exchange of gifts. The moral value

38

invested in her is an essential part of the *ema lisan's* perception of marriage and I shall return to it.

It should have become evident by now that marriage is merely one component in a complex of mutually binding rights and obligations, made possible by the exchange of women and bridewealth, that bring together descent groups or families into formal relationships. The nuclear family – the unit of kinship that engages the attention of *malai* – is only one social unit nested within a segmentary structure consisting of clans and lineages. This means that the rights and obligations that marriage establishes or maintains involve all manner of relatives, including uncles, brothers, and cousins in addition to the immediate parents-in-law. Critics of the *barlaque* have a tendency to reserve their understanding of the *folin* to money a prospective husband delivers to the bride's father but according to *lisan* it is a group affair in which brothers, uncles, and cousins contribute to a set of gifts of which money is only one element. For his part, the bride's father has the duty of redistributing the gifts among *his* kinsfolk. Father and father-in-law, as it were, act as conduits through which pass items of wealth that affect their descent groups.

Critics of the *barlaque* typically pay only cursory attention to the fact that the *barlaque* involves a *mutual exchange* of prestations. Nor do they understand the moral implications of the fact that the relationship that is defined by this exchange may endure for years after a particular marriage had been contracted. *Lisan* impels affinal partners to help one another in matters that involve ritual, economic, and political concerns. Persons related through marriage assist each other to bury their dead, for instance, and they celebrate the entrance into the human world of their affines' newly-born. As the child grows up and school fees must be paid, affines may assist with the expenses of education. Before the Portuguese pacified the kingdoms, alliance partners mounted headhunting raids together and prior to King Boaventura's submission to the Portuguese in 1912 a king's affines would support him in battles with other kings. What Schulte-Nordholt (1971: 388) has written about the Meto, '... in the case of war the bride-receiving ruler could marshal the support of his bride-giver', was true in East

39

Timor. Duarte (1964: 96–97) points out that in pre-Portuguese times the Timorese lacked a centralized political system that could maintain order among *sukus* divided by language, kinship groups, and kingdoms. Their need for survival encouraged *sukus* to join forces in mutually supportive alliances like the *fetosa-umane*.[14]

So important is the institution of generalized exchange in Timorese society that in describing how it operates among the Northern Tetum of West Timor, Ernest Brandewie and Simon Asten (1976: 19–39) go so far as to define their entire society in its terms and emphasize its transcendent role: '[...] the arrangement of *society* [my emphasis] into *fettosawa-umamane* [wife-taking/wife-giving] lineages, with the approved variations on this theme, is what stabilizes marriage, identifies and allocates children to their proper place in society, and generally organizes their social world for the Northern Belunese.' Discussing the function of marriage in societies with a structured character somewhat similar to those found in Timor, Arthur Maurice Hocart (1933: 258) remarks that '[t]he system then is not based on marriage, but marriage is regulated by the system'. So deeply entrenched in Timorese society is the *barlaque* that it exemplifies what Marcel Mauss has called a 'total social phenomenon', i.e.,

---

14 '*Conceito e sentimento que reflectem a necessidade e o instinto da própria conservação e defesa, numa sociedade primitiva, alveolar, que se axadrezava em tribus demarcadas por frontiera naturais muito ingratas, por fronteiras políticas demasiadamente frágeis e separadas entre si por uma aranheira de línguas ou dialectos e subdialectos que necessàriamente concorriam mais para dificultar do que facilitar relaçoês de boa vizinhança. Uma sociedade, assim compartimentada, tinha que se sentir bastante exposta a guerrilhas, saques e depredaçoês De sorte que, quanto mais se consolidasse e ramificasse a família, mais garantida se tornava a sua defesa, não só dentro da própria tribu, clão our reino, mas ainda além-fronteira.'* [Imagination and sentiment which reflected the necessity of self-preservation and defence in a primitive society, divided up into a network of tribes, demarcated by very vague natural boundaries, by political frontiers extremely fragile, and separated among themselves by a web of languages or dialects and sub-dialects that necessarily made it difficult to bring about good relationships. In a society thus compartmentalized, a person had to feel quite exposed to raiding, sacking, and depredations so that the more consolidated and ramified the family, the greater guaranteed was its defence, not only inside the tribe itself, clan or kingdom, but beyond the frontiers as well.]

a complex of collective representations (*représentations collectives*) that incorporate a society's most cherished values in social, political, and economic relationships, symbolism, social identity, gender, and ritual. Nor is this all. As a total social phenomenon the *barlaque* can lay claim to being regarded as a microcosm of Timorese society. As Duarte (1964: 96) puts it: 'The kinship relationship created by the institution of the *fetosa-umane* is one of affinity. But the sentiment and the obligation of solidarity it contains for all those who enter into it surpasses much more than westerners can imagine.'[15]

Just as the networks involved in the *fetosa-umane* have what might be described as a horizontal aspect linking alliance groups of the same generation, so do they also have a vertical aspect. It is not uncommon for the bridewealth to be only partly discharged by the time the wedding takes place and is only gradually discharged in stages, with the children and even grandchildren inheriting the obligation. Although generational indebtedness can endanger a family's economic wellbeing, by such 'vertical ramifications' families are assured of mutual support inter-generationally so long as the alliance lasts. Families sometimes maintain their indebtedness deliberately as a way of ensuring these social bonds continue and choose never to eradicate the debt, a practice echoing the custom in rural Ireland in the days before the Second World War when farmers would buy goods from local shopkeepers on credit and pay off only a portion of their debts after they sold their agricultural surplus. Although in a good season a farmer might be able to discharge the entire amount, he would do so only if he wanted to sever his relationship with the shopkeeper (Arensburg and Kimball 1940).

GENDER AND THE *BARLAQUE*

As to whether the *barlaque* belittles the female gender, it must be conceded that the translation of *folin* as 'price' and the expression by

---

15 '*O parentesco que se contrai, pelo instituto do feto-sá-umane, é de afinidade. Mas o sentimento e a obrigação de solidariedade, que envolve, para todos os que nele entram, superam tudo o que um ocidental possa imaginar.*'

which Timorese marriage is typically known – 'buying the bride' – implies as much because it would seem to reduce the woman to the status of a chattel and degrade the value of womanhood. But does it also, as some anti-*barlaque* proponents claim, promote violence against the wife? The following passage makes that claim:

> In many cases, the *barlaque* and the patrilocal residence associated with it contribute to gender-based violence (VBG), as well as promoting the idea of women being like property, establishes relations of unequal power in the core of the family and installs the idea that wives be subservient. (Narcisco and Henriques 2008: 10).

One can readily see why the *folin* can be construed as a payment. With 'price' among its referents and the public display of largesse displayed at the wedding of wealthy families, handing over a *folin* might seem to acknowledge as much. Yet a convincing case can be made that the *barlaque*, far from demeaning the female sex, actually enhances womanhood (*feto*) in Timorese collective thought and that women are no more 'bought' with a *folin* than men are 'bought' with a dowry.

In the first place, the *ema lisan* themselves affirm – and do so unequivocally – that wives are not bought (Hicks 2010: 121–22) and they are, after all, the women and men who practise the *barlaque* and may be expected to have a more informed understanding of it than *malai*. Secondly, the bride is not a fungible commodity substitutable by monetary value but *the* essential human and moral element in one of the most fundamental social, economic, and political relationships in Timorese society.

Therefore, and thirdly, the assertion that 'her [the bride's] family reciprocates with much lesser gifts' diminishes her status as the most important gift in this mutual exchange of prestations. Both alliance groups understand that without her gift of a new life to her husband's descent group it would be unable to reproduce itself and face extinction.[16] This acknowledgment some Timorese groups make in describing her as the 'source of life' (Clamagirand 1980: 145; Vroklage

---

16 Since in this affinal relationship the wife-giving group reciprocates with gifts given to the husband's group, it might be argued that the *barlaque* does, after

1952: 137), an image evoking a goddess-like nature rather than a commodity bought in a store in Dili. Or even a [male] player that the Lisbon soccer club, Benfica, might purchase from Manchester United for a few million pounds. As a matter of incidental note, it might be recalled that in Europe until recent times giving a dowry for the husband was customary, as it is today in countries like India. Indeed, in parts of the Western World the bride's father is still expected to foot the bill for his daughter's wedding, which can amount to an expensive dowry substitute. Would those who characterize the *barlaque* as 'buying a wife' consider this practice to be the equivalent of 'buying a husband' and demeaning men?

Fourthly, far from devaluating women the *barlaque* endows the female sex with an enviable status. If bridewealth constitutes – as it most definitely does – a major expenditure of resources from the wife-taking group to the wife-giving group, does not this suggest an extraordinarily elevated value that traditionally-minded people – women as well as men – invest in the female sex? I recall discussing marriage with a Viqueque man who had heard me say that I had not given bridewealth for my wife and being told that while *malai* had their own customs, Timorese women and men did not simply copulate like animals: Timorese men gave *folin*! Discussing this question in the context of the Tetum-speakers in West Timor, B. A. Vroklage remarks that

> [...] in the course of my researches in Belu (Central Timor) it became very clear to me that, though the people use expressions like price and purchase amount in connection with a marriage, they only mean the derivative or wider sense of price or buying in this case and they definitely do not want these expressions to be understood literally. Everywhere the idea of buying the bride was indignantly repudiated and I was told: 'The bride is not a buffalo', or 'She not an animal', or 'She is not a slave'. A woman would feel deeply insulted if one should tell her that she was bought. In Lidak and Lassiolat (regions in West Timor) they added that she would run away at once and that her husband would have to pay

---

all, involve the giving of a dowry. This claim, however, is weakened by the absence of any prominent indigenous terminological counterpart of *folin*.

a heavy fine to her family to prevail upon her to return. (Vroklage 1952: 137).[17]

Fifthly, if bridewealth amounts to a mere commercial transaction, why should it be part of a ritual, and a ritual moreover awash in symbolism? Significant stages in the marriage ceremony are identified in metaphor as are individual component gifts of the total prestation and the persons of the bride and bridegroom themselves. Writing about the Tetum of Samoro, in Manatuto district, Duarte (1964) notes that '[t]he ceremony [i.e., wedding] just described is a plethora of symbols inherent in the materials' employed, in the utensils used, in the verbal formulas uttered.'[18] Duarte (Ibid. 94) paid close attention to the symbolically-loaded language used in the Samoro marriage ritual of a *liurai*. It includes a prenuptial prestation that consists of two parts. The first part, called the *osan-cain rua*, entitles the prospective groom and his family to commence marriage negotiations (*lati odan* ['to lean against the steps' of the future bride's house]). The second part, the *osan-ulun rua*, entitles the representatives of the young man's group to enter the house to initiate bridewealth discussions and bears the appellation *core lesu-matan* or 'unfastening the cord or string of the door' (of the girl's house). These are but two illustrations from a constellation of verbal images that figuratively embellish the union of the couple. Ritual gestures and symbolic artefacts accompany the words uttered and by inviting the ancestors (*mate bein*) of both descent groups to witness the exchange, the ceremony conjoins spirits and humans. Vroklage (1952–53), too, describes the rich imagery employed in Timorese marriages and the article by Ernest Brandewie and Simon Asten

---

17 Vroklage (1952: 137) is of the opinion that the 'parts of the bride price plainly indicate what is the guiding principle of the bride price. It is a compensation for the loss of the bride, who becomes incorporated into another family group. Furthermore it is a compensation for the pain, the care, the trouble and the expense incurred for her, as well as for the sorrow of the parting, and finally is a consolation for the ancestors expressed in a valuable present.'

18 'A cerimónia que se acaba de descriver é pletórica em simbolismo: nas figuras que intervêm, na 'matéria' que se emprega, nos utensílios que se usam, no texto das fórmulas.'

(1976) on marriage actually bears the sub-title 'a study of symbols'. If the *barlaque* is simply a device for buying a wife, why would the institution be so ritualized and so replete with symbolism, some of which specifically includes images of the bride's anticipated fertility?

Luís Costa and others are, therefore, mistaken in portraying the *barlaque* merely as an exchange of 'goods' of 'equivalent value' since the bride, of course, cannot be described as 'goods' and the gifts exchanged are far from equivalent given the overwhelmingly superior value of the bride.

Sixthly, as I have pointed out earlier, critics tend to reduce this complex institution to one of marriage between two individuals and the exchange of the *folin* by the bride's father as its *raison d'être*. Yet, just as the *barlaque* amounts to considerably more than the economic materiality of gifts, so, too, does it encompass much more than marriage, especially in the *fetosa-umane* which requires that maintaining the co-operative relationship be regularly reified after the nuptials by successive gift-exchanges for as long as the alliance exists.

In 2011 the Timorese NGO, Belun, issued a policy briefing (EWER 2011) with 'Culture and its Impact on Community Life as its Theme' and it culled ethnographic data from many sub-districts in East Timor. The document provides a valuable source of data on the *barlaque* and some of its recommendations are sound. It notes the *fetosa-umane*'s contribution to community cohesion at the same time as calling attention to the economic burden that assembling the *folin* can place on some families. On the other hand, Josh Trindade (2011) –quite properly, in my opinion – remarks that among the report's shortcomings is its 'Dili based, economic, western and individualistic' perspective and its failure to acknowledge the reality of the institution's ritual aspects.[19]

What of the claim that the *barlaque* fosters domestic violence? Research comparing violence in marriages in which the *folin* is given

---

19 Trindade also takes issue with the brief's recommendation (p. 8) that the government regulate the *barlaque* by bringing it within a formal system of law. A discussion of this proposal would take me beyond my terms of discussion, but I can register my concurrence with Trindade's arguments against it.

with marriages in which it is not given would be needed for this claim to be verified or disputed and this has yet to be carried out.[20]

It appears to me that attempts by national and international agencies to instill respect for the female gender among Timorese are redundant. *Lisan* codes provide just such respect and have the weighty advantage of being indigenous.

DOES THE *BARLAQUE* HAVE A FUTURE?

As with all institutions, the *barlaque* is subject to change and will either decline into irrelevance or adapt to new circumstances as time moves on, a latter capacity it has already demonstrated. The early 20th century saw the infusion of cash into the *folin* and later the introduction of tokens of material wealth from the *malai* world, like bridal beds, mattresses, and cutlery. Protocols prescribing which categories of relatives are marriageable and which ones are not have also changed while elaborate imagery is no longer deemed a *sine qua non* of weddings. These are likely harbingers of further changes the future will bring.[21] But the *barlaque's* importance in Timorese society and the extent to which it is engrained in indigenous values suggest that despite criticism from Dili-centric Timorese and *malai* the institution is unlikely to disappear.

What might these further changes be?[22] I suspect that as the *ema lisan* become increasingly aware of alternative ways of defining social

---

20 Josh Trindade (2011) argues against the claim that it incites violence against women and an important study based on interviews of women of different generations in and outside Dili conducted by Sara Niner (2012) reveals the ambiguity educated women have about the *barlaque* as it relates to gender equality, domestic violence against women, and commercial implications. She discusses the different consequences that result from giving or not giving the *folin* whether by families living in a patrilineal community who simply choose to ignore the conventions and refuse to give it, and among matrilineal communities where giving the *folin* is not part of their *lisan*. Her article includes an extensive and highly useful list of sources on the *barlaque*.

21 The question of whether the *ema lisan* should change their traditional values to align them with those currently valued by *malai* is, of course, a separate issue.

22 The following remarks should not be taken as prescriptive suggestions. The future of Timor-Leste is the business of the Timorese, Dili-centred and *ema*

relationships individuals may become more conscious of their status as citizens and feel less loyalty to their descent groups and their *lisan*. With this change in attitude, both lateral dimensions and vertical dimensions of the *fetosa-umane* may be expected to undergo contraction and with this contraction kinship and affinal duties will cease to be as mandatory as they are at present. As the compulsive grip, now wielded by descent groups over their members, gradually eases, so may society become increasing atomized with the nuclear family replacing the descent group as the most influential kinship unit and agency in marriage. Individuals may be less impelled to define themselves exclusively in terms of descent and while the ancestors may be expected to retain influence they may be gradually supplanted by 'international attitudes', among which the notion that education for girls is every bit as essential as for boys will be especially consequential.[23]

In part as a consequence of these adjustments I think that although the *folin* will continue to maintain its position as the contractual centerpiece of most forms of the *barlaque*, its size will contract to more modest dimensions. Not necessarily in all marriages – wealthy families will continue to take pride in the public display of the impressive resources they command – but social expectations that the 'generic' bridewealth should amount to a substantial proportion of a family's wealth may be supplanted by a preference to invest resources in the

---

lisan alike, not the *malai*, and my thoughts about how the *barlaque* might evolve do not reflect any preference I might have about what the future might bring. The republic is already graced by an over-abundance of foreigners only too willing to instruct Timorese in how they should live their lives.

23 In an interview, Mr. Agustinho Caet, Languages Advisor of the Ministry of Education, made a certain comment worthy of attention. He declared that many women never complete their education but marry early because they are an economic asset to their parents. While noting that '[t]his does not happen in all the districts', he said that, 'in some districts parents get very happy when they have many daughters because they reflect the money they will get for them through the Barlaki (dowry) system [sic]'. He went on to say that 'according to some traditions, women do not need to get a high level education. When a man wants to marry someone's daughter, the parents will remove their daughter from school.' Mr. Caet added that 'some parents give more importance to the Barlaki and how much money they will get for their daughters than with their level of education' (Caet 2011).

individual's own family rather than redistribute it to affines with whom, in any case, reciprocal ties may have become more attenuated.

Finally, these social and economic modifications to the *barlaque* might have an aesthetic correspondent in the spiritual realm as the institution's symbolism becomes less elaborate and no longer makes incessant symbolic statements about the life-giving fertility of women and the power of the ancestors to facilitate it but remain only as evocative vestiges of a past.

Since the value that womanhood already has in the context of the *barlaque* as the institution currently functions is not inconsistent with international values and assuming the adaptations described above come to pass, I see no reason why this critical institution will not continue to play a role in Timor-Leste society. Nor need it prove to be an obstacle to the *ema lisan* becoming as conscious of themselves as citizens of a modern nation-state as they are of being kin and affines.[24] In light of the above considerations, those hostile to the *barlaque* – educated Timorese and *malai* alike – might take a moment to remember that the nation-state has been in existence only since 2002 but the *barlaque* has been around for generations.

REFERENCES

The American Heritage Dictionary of the English Language. 1992. Third Edition. Boston, New York, London: Houghton Mifflin Company.

Arensburg, C. M. and S. T. Kimball. 1940. *Family and Community in Ireland.* Cambridge, Mass: Harvard University Press.

---

24 In the case of some families that identify with Dili, the future, as it were, appears to have arrived, or perhaps almost arrived. In her instructive account of how marriages are contracted in the capital, Kelly Silva (2010: 126–28) has described the various interpretations of the *barlaque* that are possible and draws attention to the institutional and moral confusions attending social change, which, as one might expect, are affecting the capital rather than *ema lisan*. These uncertainties will surely occur in the *foho* when more 'Dili values' are assimilated by the *ema lisan*.

Brandewie, Ernest and Simon Asten. 1976. 'Northern Belunese (Tetum) Marriage and Kinship: A Study of Symbols'. *Philippine Quarterly of Culture and Society* 4: 19–30.

Caet, A. 'Gender: Women Represent an Economic Asset for the Parents'. Interview by Isabella Ermelita, conducted on October 11, 2011. *The Dili Weekly*, January 3, 2012. www.thediliweekly.com/.

Clamagirand, B. 1980. 'The Social Organization of the Ema of Timor'. In Fox, James J. (ed.) *The Flow of Life: Essays on Eastern Indonesia*. Harvard University Press, pp. 314–51.

Corrêa, Armando Pinto. 1935. *Gentio de Timor*. Lisboa: Lucas.

Costa, Luís. 2000. Colaboração Ténica Margarita Correia. *Dicionário de Tétum-Português*. Lisbon: Faculdade de Letras, Universidade de Lisboa, Edições Colibri.

Cunningham, Clark. 1967. 'Atoni Kin Categories and Conventional Behaviour'. *Bijdragen Tot de Taal-, Land- en Volkenkunde* 123: 53–70.

Duarte, J. B. 1964. '*Barlaque: Casamento Gentílico Timorense*'. Seara 11 (*nova série*), May–Agosto, No. 3–4: 92–119, 1964 (August).

Evans-Pritchard, E. E. 1931. 'An alternative Term for "Bride-Price"'. *Man* Vol. 31, (Mar., 1931), pp. 36–9. www.jstor.org/stable/2789533.

EWER [Early Warning Early Response]. 2011. Policy Briefing No. 5. *Culture and Its Impact on*

Social and Community Life: A Case Study of Timor Leste. Author: Constantino da C. C. X. Escollano Brandao. Editors: Eunchim Choi, Marilia Oliveira da Costa, Sarah Dewhurst, Luis Ximenes. New York: Center for International Conflict Resolution, Columbia University, 2011.

Forbes, H. O. 1884. 'On Some of the Tribes of the Island of Timor'. *Journal of the Royal Anthropological Institute* 13: 402–31.

Forth, Gregory L. 1981. *Rindi: an ethnographic study of a traditional domain in Eastern Sumba*. The Hague: Martinus Nijhoff.

Hicks, David. 1973. 'The Cairui and Uai Ma'a of Timor'. *Anthropos* 68: 473–8l.

—— 1978. 'Structure and Change: A Relationship Terminology in Transition'. In *Structural Analysis in Anthropology: Case Studies from Indonesia and Brazil*. Studia Instituti Anthropos. *Volume 30*. Pp. 113–25. St. Augustin bei Bonn, Germany.

—— 1981. 'A Two Section System with Matrilineal Descent among the Tetum of Eastern Indonesia'. *Sociologus, n. s.* 31 (2): 181–84.

—— 1983. 'A Transitional Relationship Terminology of Asymmetric Prescriptive Alliance among the Makassai of Eastern Indonesia'. *Sociologus, n. s.* 33 (1): 73–85.

—— 1986. 'The Relationship Terminology of the Ema'. *Sociologus, n.s.* 36 (2): 162–71.

—— 1987. 'Cognation and Generalized Exchange'. *Sociologus, n.s.* 37 (2): 177–80.

—— 1989. 'Confirmations and Corrections: Tetum Terms of Relationship from Central Timor'. *Sociologus, n.s.* 39 (2): 153–60.

—— 1990. *Kinship and Religion in Eastern Indonesia. Gothenburg Studies in Social Anthropology. Volume 12.* Gothenburg, Sweden: Acta Universitatis Gothoburgensis.

—— 2004. *Tetum Ghosts and Kin: Fertility and Gender in East Timor.* Long Grove, Illinois: Waveland Press, Inc. Second edition. (First edition: 1976).

—— 2007. 'The Naueti Relationship Terminology: a new instance of asymmetric prescription from Timor'. *Bijdragen Tot de Taal-, Land- en Volkenkunde* 163 (2/3): 239–62.

—— 2010. 'The Barlaque of Timor-Leste'. In *Transition, Society and Politics in Timor-Leste,* edited by Paulo Castro Seixas. Porto: Universidade Fernando Pessoa. Pp. 115–22.

—— 2012. 'Compatibility, Resilience and Adaptation: the *barlaque* of Timor-Leste'. *Local-Global: Identity, Security, Community. Volume 11.* Special Edition, edited by Damian Grenfell. Pp. 124–37.

Hocart, Arthur Maurice. 1933. *The Progress of Man: A Short Survey of His Evolution, His Customs, and His Works.* London: Methuen.

Hull, Geoffrey. 1999. *Standard Tetum–English Dictionary*. St. Leonards, New South Wales, Australia: Allen & Unwin in association with the University of Western Sydney Macarthur.

Leach, Edmund. 1951. 'The Structural Implications of Matrilateral Cross-Cousin Marriage'. *Journal of the Royal Anthropological Institute* 81: 23–55.

Lévi-Strauss, Claude. 1949. *Les structures élémentaires de la parenté*. Paris: Presses Universitaires de France.

Mauss, Marcel. 1968. *Oeuvres: 1. Les fonctions sociales du sacré*. V. Karady (ed.) Paris: Les éditions de Minuit.

Mendes, P. M. 1935. *Dicionário Tetum-Português*. Dili: Fernandes e Filhos Ltas.

Narcisco, V. and P. D. de Sousa Henriques. 2008. 'O Papel das Mulheres no Desenvolvimento Rural: Uma leitura para Timor-Leste'. CEFAGE-UE Working Paper 2008/04. CEFAGE-UE, Universidade de Évora, Largo dos Colegiais 2, 7000-803 Évora, Portugal. Web page: www.cefage.uevora.pt.

Needham, Rodney. 1960. 'Alliance and Classification among the Lamet'. *Sociologus* 10:97–119.

—— 1962. *Structure and Sentiment: a test case in social anthropology*. Chicago: Chicago University Press.

Niner, Sara L. 2012. '*Barlake:* An exploration of marriage practices and issues of women's status in Timor-Leste'. 2012. *Local–Global: Security, Community, 11,* pp. 138–153.

The Oxford University Dictionary. Second Edition, Volume IV: Creel-Duzepere 2000 (1989). Prepared by J. A. Simpson and E. S. C. Weiner.

Rodgers, Susan. 1984. 'Orality, Literacy, and Batak Concepts of Marriage Alliance'. *Journal of Anthropological Research* 40 (3): 434–50.

Sá, Artur Basílio de. 1961. *Textos em Teto Literatura Oral Timorense*. Lisbon: Junta de Investigaçoês.

Schulte-Nordholt, H. G. 1971. *The Political System of the Atoni of Timor*. Translated from the Dutch by M. J. L. van Yperen. The Hague: Martinus Nijhoff.

Silva, Kelly. 2010. '*Foho* Versus Dili: the political role of place in East Timor'. In *Transition, Society and Politics in Timor-Leste*, edited by Paulo Castro Seixas. Porto: Universidade Fernando Pessoa. Pp. 123–36.

da Silva, Lourenço Marques. 2003. *Barlake Tuir Lisan Emar Makasae-Soba: estudu deskritivu estruturál no aprosimasaun semiótika*. Dili: Universidade Nacionál Timór Lorosa'e, Faculdade de Ciências da Educação, Instituto Nasional Linguística nian Liceu Dr. Francisco Machado, Díli Timor Leste.

Sousa, I. C. 2001. 'The Portuguese Colonization and the Problem of East Timorese Nationalism'. *Lusotopie*: 183–94.

Trindade, Josh. Email correspondence dated October 13, 2011. jtrindade76@hotmail.com.

Vroklage, B. A. G. 1952. 'Bride Price or Dower'. *Anthropos* 47: 133–46.

——— 1952–1953. *Ethnographie der Belu in Zentral-Timor*, Three volumes. Leiden: E. J. Brill.

Wallace, Alfred Russel. 1869. *The Malay Archipelago: The Land of the Orang-utan and the Bird of Paradise, a Narrative of Travel, with Studies of Man and Nature*. Two volumes. London: Macmillan and Co.

Wouden, F. A. E. van 1935. *Sociale Structuurtypen in de Groote Oost*. Leiden: J. Ginsberg.

CHAPTER 4

Making The King Divine
A Case Study in Ritual Regicide from Timor

Nous avons vu qu'entre la victime et le dieu il y a toujours quelque affinité ... C'est par le semblable qu'on nourrit le semblable et la victime est la nourriture des dieux. Aussi le sacrifice a-t-il été rapidement considéré comme la condition même de l'existence divine. C'est lui qui fournit la matière immortelle dont vivent les dieux (Hubert and Mauss 1898: 129–30).

A central feature of Durkheim's thesis regarding the origin of religion was his argument that the concept of a divinity as a 'category of understanding' owed its genesis to dispositions aroused by human beings coming together in ritual (1960: 420–21). Repetitions of ritual performances, he concluded, renewed these dispositions. As Bloch (1986: 7) puts it, 'Durkheim sees ritual as the device by which the categories of understanding organising our perception of nature and of society are created and given their categorical, hence inevitable, and compulsive nature'. Durkheim appears to have been uncertain about the process by which this might occur;[1] yet, curiously, 13 years earlier in their work on sacrifice, his collaborators on the *Année Sociologique,* Hubert and Mauss (1898), had come close to hinting at one possibility.

---

1 Evans-Pritchard (1965: 64, 68), for one, dismissed Durkheim's causation theory of religion as merely a form of 'crowd psychology'. 'He is claiming that spirit, soul, and other religious ideas and images are projections of society, or of its segments, and originate in conditions bringing about a state of effervescence ... fundamentally Durkheim elicits a social fact from crowd psychology' (Ibid.: 68). For further elaboration of this approach, see Lukes (1985: 462–65, 483) who has also alerted us to Durkheim's failure to appreciate the complexity of the social realities to which religious phenomena relate and his tendency to accord them a greater unitary character than they actually possess.

Hubert and Mauss claimed to have isolated as the defining element of sacrifice the communication between the 'profane' and 'sacred' brought about by the consecration of a victim whom the act destroyed. They appear to have thought that the exemplary sacrifice was that of a god who, through unqualified self-abnegation, offers himself to humankind, in this way bestowing the benefit of life, or a revival of life, upon mortals. At the same time, Hubert and Mauss recognized that the gods whom human beings create also have needs (*la matière immortelle*). It is therefore all the more unexpected that in seeking to disclose what has been referred to as the 'grammar' of sacrificial rituals (Evans-Pritchard 1964: viii), they seem to have ignored the opposite, yet complementary, mode of sacrifice in which a representative of humanity offers his or her life up for the benefit of divinity. The Word might become Flesh, so to speak; but the Flesh might also become the Word.

In this chapter I propose one possible way in which the sacrifice of a human figure representing a deity might operate as a strategy for evoking the concept of god. To this end, I shall try to combine Durkheim's equation of god and society with certain insights derived from Hubert and Mauss.[2] The figure considered here is known to anthropologists as 'the divine king'.

The term 'divine king' is, of course, open to various interpretations (see Feeley-Harnik 1985; Needham 1980: 66–78; Young 1966: 135–36). Some idea of the diversity of the attributes and powers of divine kings and the advantages to be gained from the use of a more generalizing term such as 'sacred king' or 'sacred chief', can be gauged from the collection of articles edited by de Heusch (1990b) whose own contribution (1990a) argues in favour of discarding this over-restrictive and culture-bound designation. However, the term 'divine king' has become well entrenched in the anthropological

---

2 Cf. de Heusch (1985: 1–25) for an evaluative overview of Hubert and Mauss's work on sacrifice in light of African ritual, including Evans-Pritchard's (1956) study of Nuer sacrifice in which, he points out, the author made his thesis conform to Hubert and Mauss's schema.

literature, and I shall adhere to the convention for the purposes of this chapter.[3]

There are also many critiques of Durkheim's theories of the sociological nature of belief and ritual, and of Hubert and Mauss's thesis on sacrifice. Valeri (1985: 65), for example, in explicating Hawaiian kingship and sacrifice, has sought to resolve the problem of the relationship between reciprocity and inequality in the sacrificial oblation: why, as he puts it, do human beings seem to give little in exchange for much? I shall return to Valeri's position later, though by way of rehearsal I might note that my own findings tend to support his argument that sacrifice creates a bond of 'mutual indebtedness' between the human and the divine (Valeri 1985: 66–67) rather than, as Durkheim, Hubert and Mauss seem to imply, a hierarchical relationship. On the contrary, I shall analyse here a ritual in which god, 'society', and the scapegoat figure of the divine king become merged by the ritual performance itself into a single moral entity in which any sense of hierarchy has been effaced.[4]

DISJUNCTION AND CONJUNCTION AT BEMALAI

Adjoining each other in central Timor are two ethno-linguistic groups, the Tetum and the Kemak (or Ema).[5] Their languages are

3   See also Beidelman (1966), Carlson (1993), Evans-Pritchard (1948), Richards (1969), Young (1966) and Vaughan (1987). Beidelman's review of 'sacrifice and sacred rule' in Africa (1987) complements that of Feeley-Harnik (1985) – as well as providing Robertson Smith with the credit often withheld from him.

4   Girard (1992) has also recently raised doubts about these three scholars' assumptions, for while he considers their emphasis on the sociological function of the sacrifice to be justified, he like Muller (1980) insists that it is a scapegoating device whose character is essentially violent. Hubert and Mauss's addiction to a diachronic style of analysis has been reassessed by de Heusch who has called into question 'their ambition' to reduce all sacrifice to a rites of passage model based on a vague typology contrasting profane and sacred (de Heusch 1985: 15, 213). As I try to demonstrate in this chapter, this model is by no means incompatible with a sacrificial ritual; but de Hensch's objection offers a salutary *caveat*.

5   One of the largest ethnic groups on Timor, the Tetum, are usually classified into three branches: the northern, southern and eastern (Hicks 1984: 7).

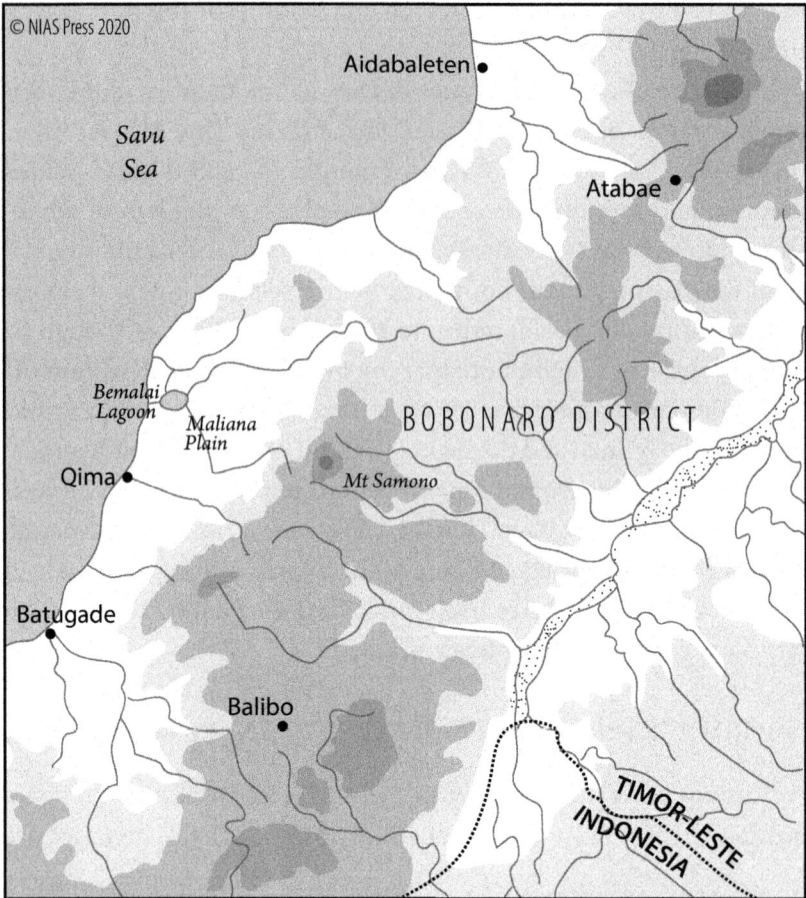

Map 2 The Bemalai Lagoon and its environs.

distinct but share many lexical features and are congeners within the wider Austronesian linguistic family. However, the closest resemblances between the two peoples can be seen at the ideational and institutional levels. These resemblances include a dualistic mode of organizing important symbolic categories such as human being/spirit, masculine/feminine, dry/wet and dry season/wet season; a supreme dual godhead comprised of a father god and a mother god; a belief in *lulik*; a conception of human existence as cyclical; a hierarchy of ranks

My own fieldwork was among the eastern branch, but I have not drawn on my data on this population for the present analysis.

including chiefs of various categories; asymmetric alliance between established sets of affines; and marriages in which wife-takers give buffaloes to their wife-givers who reciprocate with pigs (Brandewie & Asten 1976; Cinatti 1965; Clamagirand 1980; Grijzen 1904; Renard-Clamagirand 1982; Vroklage 1952; Wortelboer 1952).[6]

Along the north coast of central Timor lies a lagoon known as Bemalai (Map 2).[7] It is approximately two kilometres long and one kilometre wide and abounds in fish and crustaceans as well as being the haunt of crocodiles. Near it lie two villages – one Tetum-speaking and the other Ema-speaking – that share a common history and narratives telling of a bloody rivalry over the lagoon's resources. With the passage of time this violence seems to have become channelled into a co-operative, yet also competitive, calendrical ritual called the *sau-biu*[8] at the climax of which a surrogate of the king of one village (Balibo) is symbolically done to death and then restored to life (King 1965: 111–12). The two communities in question are Balibo, which is inhabited by comparatively recent Tetum immigrants to the region, and the Ema village of Atabae, whose people comprise the autochthonous population.[9] The two otherwise disjunctive communities conjoin into a single social entity every few years when their inhabitants converge on Bemalai, whose resources each village continues to claim as its own, and express their shared ideas and institutions in a performance of the *sau-biu* ritual.

Our principal authorities on the Northern Tetum are Brandewie and Asten (1976), Grijzen (1904), Vroklage (1952) and Wortelboer

---

6 All quotations from Renard-Clamagirand (1982) and Cinatti (1965) are my translations.

7 *Be* + *malai*. In the Tetum language, *be* or *we* = 'liquid', 'water', 'source', 'point of origin'. The corresponding Ema term is *bea* (Renard-Clamagirand 1982: 230). *Malai*, of course, connotes 'stranger' or 'foreigner'.

8 *Sau'* (*n*) = the lifting of a ritual interdiction; the meaning of *biu* has not been recorded. The ritual continued to be enacted until at least well into the early Twenty-First Century.

9 Balibo lies about 10 kilometers southeast of the lagoon; Atabae lies about 16 kilometres to the northeast.

Plate 9 The Bemalai Lagoon in the dry season
of 2005. Photo: Maxine Hicks.

(1952). Renard-Clamagirand[10] is our only authority on the Ema. Although their respective ethnographies do not specifically deal with these two villages – Renard-Clamagirand's fieldwork was carried out at Marobo, a community southeast of Bemalai, while the (exiguous) reports by other authors refer to the Tetum region as a whole – they are nevertheless consistent with the data reported from Bemalai, such differences as may occur being variations in mutually shared beliefs and practices rather than radical differences. Thus, whereas in one ritual carried out at Marobo the rainy season is opened by the blowing of a horn (Renard-Clamagirand 1982: 290), in the equivalent Bemalai ritual it is signalled by dancing, shouting and singing (King 1965: 115). The concept of a source from which human life originates is reified at Marobo as an altar with a bamboo arising from it (Renard-Clamagirand 1982: 270–71) and, at Bemalai, as an altar comprised of a tree trunk with a fishing net cast around it. This tree trunk represents the sacred banyan tree (*ficus indica*) that stands in the centre of every

---

10 Renard-Clamagirand and Clamagirand denote the same person. Except when specifically citing works published under the name Clamagirand, I refer to this author as Renard-Clamagirand.

ancestral village[11] (Cinatti 1965: 40). In fundamental socio-cultural particulars, however, Marobo and Atabae are unquestionably part of the same tradition. As for Balibo, data relating to that village suggest that it is an entirely typical northern Tetum village.

The published ethnography on the Bemalai ritual consists of Cinatti (1965), King (1963; 1965) and Vondra (1968). My analysis is based upon their findings, supplemented by data from Pascoal (1967) and Duarte (n.d.; personal communication). The latter, during research that I carried out among Timorese refugees in Lisbon, kindly permitted me access to an unpublished Bemalai text that he had collected in the field.[12]

Since all these accounts describe ritual performances during the 1960s, this decade will serve as my 'ethnographic present'.

The purposes of the ritual, as stated by Timorese, are 'to commemorate the myth of the creation of Bemalai' (King 1965: 110), to 'recreate the myth' (King 1965: 111), and to 'ensure a continuation of an abundant supply of fish' (Cinatti 1965: 110).[13] The sacrifice also 'lifts the prohibitions prescribed by the sacred character of the lagoon' (Cinatti 1965: 41). Shared assumptions about fecundity, gender, hierarchy, political and spiritual authority, asymmetric alliance and matters of cosmology enable the two communities to transcend their socio-cultural individualities and achieve, albeit temporarily, a com-

---

11 Cinatti (1965: 34) has a photograph of the *lia na'in* reciting the Bemalai narratives under a banyan tree.

12 The ethnographic data from Bemalai, it might be noted, lend themselves to interpretation from several alternative perspectives including the ecological and political, as well as the structural, in addition to suggesting insights into several anthropological problems such as the theoretical relationship between ritual and narrative (see Hicks 1992).

13 Since I am dependent upon the reports of other authors, it might be worth remarking that in my discussions concerning Bemalai with Duarte, who as a Timorese was very familiar with Bemalai, he ventured no misgivings of any kind about the accuracy of Cinatti's depiction of the ritual – or indeed of any of the others – and that although there are some minor differences of ethnographic detail between the five authors, there is a general – indeed quite striking – concordance on all substantial matters of fact and interpretation.

mon identity as a unified collectivity headed by a single ruler. These considerations find ritual expression in symbols (gestures, words and objects) employed to transform this ruler, whose local eminence merits the designation of 'king', into his divine counterpart, the 'lord of the water' (*we na'in*). The sacrifice of the king's blood regenerates this divinity (and the spirit world in general) thereby inducing the spirit world to reciprocate with the gift of fecundity and bringing advantages to divinity and mortals alike. It is an 'operation whereby the Timorese establish a relationship with the sacred spirit ... thus utilizing benefits which before were prohibited' (Ibid.: 51).

In their interpretation of Tetum social and symbolic categories,[14] Brandewie and Asten (1976: 19) emphasize 'the dualistic character of [the Tetum] outlook' and 'the implications of alliance and of dualism' in the Tetum 'social world' and 'symbol-world'. The fact that Asten is himself a Tetum person adds a special authority to their contentions and Renard-Clamagirand (1982) is equally insistent about the pervasiveness of dualism as an organizing principle among the Ema. Inevitably, therefore, the Bemalai ritual exploits this dualistic form of classification and in doing so elaborates the important notion that for the Timorese human experience can be conceived of as incorporating a cyclical movement between human and spiritual modes of existence.

Although the contrast between human being and spirit does not appear to find explicit expression in indigenous terminology, the term *ema* in the Tetum language is glossed by Brandewie and Asten (1976: 19) as 'man' or 'people', by which they evidently mean 'human being'. It is also the self-referencing designation used by the Ema (Clamagirand 1980: 135). However, while there is a Tetum term *hu*, which encompasses the notions of 'spirit' and 'breath' (Duarte 1964: 104), neither language apparently includes a generic term for spirit beings. Nevertheless, as we shall see, the conceptual contrast between 'human being' and 'spirit' finds continual expression in ritual action and verbally in narrative among both groups (Grijzen 1904; Renard-Clamagirand 1982).

---

14 Cf. Chapter 3.

The interaction between the denizens of a visible world inhabited by human beings and those of an invisible world inhabited by spirits is critical in Tetum and Ema cosmologies (Grijzen 1904: 74–86; Renard-Clamagirand 1982). While the abode of the spirits may be variously described as underground, across the sea, in the sky, or on top of a mountain, both populations regard it as the source of life, fertility and prosperity. Ritual, like the Bemalai ceremony, provides the instrument by which humans can access this source (Grijzen 1904: 74–80; Renard-Clamagirand 1982: 291) and narrative shows how this might be done. In narrative the water divinity is usually hypostasized as a crocodile or large fish ailing from some injury which is cured by a human being who enters the spiritual world, restores vigour to the divinity, and then returns to the human world. Such is the plot of two narratives recited at Bemalai (see Duarte n. d.; Pascoal 1967: 132–37). The moment of transformation in both directions is typically affected by the hero closing his eyes as though dying and opening them as though revivified – precisely as does the human victim who 'dies' and is 'restored to life' in the ritual of regicide.

After being revitalized, the deity rewards the hero with a herd of buffaloes that miraculously keeps growing. Duarte's text stipulates that the pig and buffalo killed during the ritual of regicide be female, thereby confirming the femininity–fertility association so strongly emphasized by Renard-Clamagirand (1982: 269). As though to reinforce this connection the narrative enjoins that the buffalo be dispatched by a spear thrust through the vaginal opening.[15]

For both populations at Bemalai, images of fertility, femininity and water are combined in the institution of asymmetric alliance. As was implied in the previous chapter, this institution, like the existential cycle itself, is conceived of in terms of 'an image of a flow of life which circulates by means of women' (Clamagirand 1980: 145), an Ema metaphor which Fox (1980: 12–13) renders as 'the idea of a return

---

15 Precept and practice may not always coincide; and in the event it does not, and a male buffalo is sacrificed, the beast is immolated by a sword thrust in in its left side, that is, its 'female side', in this way maintaining the feminine connotations of the sacrifice.

or reunion of life', and one whose Tetum counterpart is the image of a stream of water flowing downhill or of water in a canal surrounding and linking different areas of a rice field (Brandwie and Asten 1976: 21). Just as the canal enables the water to flow, so does the affinal bond enable the life which women nurture to be transmitted from wife-givers to wife-takers (Ibid.; Clamagirand 1980: 145).

To perpetuate the cycle, the people of Bemalai procure the resources of life, fertility and prosperity from their god at the same time as they infuse energy into this being.[16] When human beings carry out rituals to replenish themselves and their divinity they seek life, fertility and prosperity where they also find death. As Renard-Clamagirand (1982: 293) phrases it: '[T]he rites tend to renew the sacred time of the origins of the community so that, replenished at the source, it can perpetuate itself'. The connection between the world of the living and that of the dead is made at places that link the two worlds (Grijzen 1904: 75–78). Among the Ema, according to Renard-Clamagirand (1982), this principally takes place at the altar, which is a 'symbol of gushing life ... a point of contact between the world of the dead and that of the living ...' (Renard-Clamagirand 1982: 270–71).

THE RITUAL

Until the 1950s the *sau-biu* used to be performed every August (Duarte 1989) at the time of transition from dry season to wet season (Cinatti 1965: 32). Just as water is associated with femininity and fertility, so is rain considered 'fecund and logically associated with 'Woman' who is the source of life' (Renard-Clamagirand 1982: 296). Since dryness is associated with males, the climatic transition may be interpreted as a transition from the masculine half of the year to the feminine half of the year.

---

16 The Ema make an association between the recent past and 'the transmission of life via the vital energy released and recirculated at death while mythical time is associated with the source of vital energy which supplies 'extra' life to reactivate the life cycle' (Clamagirand 1980: 150).

Preparations for the ritual begin when villagers notice dead fish and prawns floating in the water. These are believed to indicate a 'waning' of the water's *lulik,* which in this context refers to its vitality or spiritual energy. Since life is thought to issue from divinity, this ebbing of nature's vitality is construed as a sign that the water divinity – as in the narratives – requires revitalization (King 1965: 110).

The man selected as the king's surrogate (ordinarily a member of the same descent group as the Balibo ruler) must be a healthy adult in whom the generative forces of masculinity are self-evident. The surrogate king is joined at the altar by two female animals and the image conveyed is one of life-sustaining fertility and reproduction brought about by the conjunction of the two genders.

A priest (corresponding to Hubert and Mauss's *sacrificateur*) from Balibo selects the day on which the ritual is to commence. On the final day before the ritual workers from both communities begin constructing a bridge across the lagoon to facilitate movement between the two groups. Then, as the sun begins to set, distinctions of precedence in ethnicity are set aside as aristocrats and commoners of the two villages intermingle in boisterous camaraderie beside the water until dawn.

The surrogate king meanwhile retires some distance away to a hut constructed specially for this occasion. Once inside, he is no longer permitted to hold conversation with anyone, nor to eat or drink (King 1965: 113); his seclusion, I suggest, signals a condition of liminality between the world of humans and that of spirits.

Ritual and narrative at Bemalai put the contrast between silence and noise to symbolic use, and noise is a marker between temporal periods, separating the wet season from the dry season and evoking notions of the regeneration of nature (cf. Renard-Clamagirand 1982: 233, 290). Accordingly, when on the following morning attendants escort the surrogate king to the water's edge, silence prevails. Some participants gather there while others congregate around the altar where the human victim awaits his deification. He kneels at the centre of the net, holding a wooden sceptre, while behind him the sacrificer, staff in hand, pretends to strike the surrogate king a blow on the head. As the victim slumps to the ground in simulated death, his hands are tied together, his sceptre is wrapped up in the fishing net, and cloth is bundled under his head as is done with a corpse being prepared for burial. This 'burial' incorporates him into the world of the spirits, and his entry there revives the moribund water god in whose identity he is apotheosized. As god, the king is at this moment the spirit of a culture hero who appears in a narrative that I shall shortly introduce (Cinatti 1965: 40).

The pig is now metonymically identified with the human sacrifice by being brought close to the dead king and the identification is metaphorically reinforced by the sacrificer plunging a knife into the creature's heart. The silence continues as the sacrificer squeezes blood from the wound into the lagoon, in an act called 'giving to the [lord of the] water' (King 1965: 113).

No sooner has the flow of blood ceased than ethnic and social distinctions reassert themselves with the appearance of a fleet of decorated boats. These slip out from the bank and move in a cortège across the surface of the water. Nobles from Balibo occupy the leading boat, a ceremonial craft, which is followed by a more utilitarian craft at whose prow stands a fisherman, net in hand, ready to cast. The helmsmen guide the vessels gently to ensure that the water is not disturbed unduly nor the silence vitiated. Commoners from Balibo crowd silently into other boats. When the boat carrying the leading fisherman has lined up behind the one containing the nobles, the fisherman slings out his net. As fishermen in the other vessels follow suit, the nobles of Atabae put out in their boats and begin competing with those of Balibo to catch fish. Commoners unable to clamber into the boats swarm from the banks into the shallows, dancing, shouting and singing 'to stir up the mud and make the fish drunk' (King 1965: 115). This cacophony of noise brings the period of silence to an end.

Each time he nets fish, a fisherman exultantly cries out 'bal'balum bal'balum' ('my part') to the god, in this way asserting humanity's rights to the catch (perhaps an analogy here between the king 'caught' in the net and the fish being netted?) and with that right established, the men of Balibo and Atabae continue their rivalry over the next few days in a furious spate of non-stop fishing, while their womenfolk watch from the bank.

For Ema and Tetum alike, breath symbolizes the transmission of life, fertility, and prosperity from spirits to human beings (Clamagirand 1980: 144; Duarte 1964: 109; Renard-Clamagirand 1982: 274, 286). Consistent with this symbolic function, as the seasonal transition is accomplished, the sacrificer breathes into the mouth of the king, infusing life into him, thereby revitalizing him, and returning him to his human condition.

The second liminal period now begins. The surrogate king has been removed from the spiritual world, but not yet reintegrated into that of humanity. As a step towards this, the sacrificer cuts the bonds restraining the victim as soon as the first fish has been netted and, freed from his constraints, the surrogate king struggles into a squatting position. Taking pains to keep his back to the water (his domain when he was a god, but now alien territory), the surrogate king places the staff, which in the meantime has been snapped in two, under the net. Bovensiepen's remarks (Chapter 1, page 16) concerning the danger involved in too close a proximity between human and spirit are worth recalling here. With eyes downcast, he follows the sacrificer who, with arms horizontally extended, carries an unsheathed ceremonial sword on his upturned palms as he steps over to the banyan tree. Here, the third, and final, sacrifice is to be offered. In it, human being and beast are made symbolically equivalent, while the principles of masculinity and femininity are conjoined. As the surrogate king sits down near the beast, the sacrificer places some areca and betel on the buffalo's tongue with the tip of his sword and then offers some to the man, who stuffs it into his mouth. Offering betel and areca is a common Tetum and Ema procedure for contacting spirits (cf. Grijzen 1904: 77; Renard-Clamagirand 1982: 277). As the sacrificer backs away, the king chews for a few moments before spitting out betel juice several times. He continues chewing as the priest thrusts a sword into the vaginal opening of the buffalo.

After butchering the carcass, and obedient to the protocols of status and hierarchy, the sacrificer sets aside a certain portion of the meat for himself and then allocates equal portions to the participants from Balibo (King 1965: 116). The king and his family are privileged to eat their portions first.[17] Since the king of Bemalai does not only literally feed his people by providing the buffalo he shares a common identity with the beast.[18] This moment in the ritual seems to correspond to Feeley-Harnik's juncture at which 'ritual and politics meet in food' (1985: 288), and recalls her argument that the Fijian stranger-king offers local residents 'cooked men', that is, sacrificial victims, to consume. The surrogate king now brings the ritual to an end, and becomes reincorporated into the human world by tossing the entrails of the buffalo into the water 'as an offering' to nourish the water god (Vondra 1968: 47). Having done this, he can now walk along the bank, mix with other human beings, and freely accept betel-chew, fish and tobacco.

Sitting with his back against the banyan (the symbolic roots of the social collectivity of Bemalai community), a local 'lord of the word' (*lia na'in*) narrates two complementary narrative that describe the origins of the lagoon, the water god, and the ritual itself (Cinatti 1965: 39–40; King 1965: 111).

Narrative 1

On behalf of their respective peoples two great chiefs from Atabae and Balibo attempted to negotiate a common boundary between their two groups, but failed to reach agreement and began brawling. As they were clubbing each other with staffs, a woman came along carrying a water jar on her head. One man – or perhaps the two of them together[19] – knocked it off, breaking the container

---

17 See Sahlins's characterization of the stranger-king of Fiji as the 'feeder of the people and their food ... the sacred ... chief [who is] domesticated ritually' by dying and being reborn (1983: 87). In this context it might be recalled that the king of Bemalai belongs to what is considered to be the immigrant population.

18 Cf. Girard: 'The sacred king is also a monster. He is simultaneously god, man and savage beast' (1992: 252).

19 In King's account (King 1965: 111) the culprit is the Balibo man; in Vondra's it is the man from Atabae (Vondra 1968: 46).

in half. The spilt water formed a lagoon, which separated the two men and formed the boundary between their two communities.

This narrative explains how the split between the people of Balibo and the people of Atabae came about, a disjunction analogous to the separation of the dry season from the wet season (cf. Renard-Clamagirand 1982: 296). It also highlights the discord which, by breaking the jar and spilling the water, today separates the hitherto homogeneous topographic and ethno-linguistic landscapes. It should also be pointed out that the narrative, with its references to a 'super-abundance' of water, is narrated at a time of year when the rains of the (always unreliable) wet season are anxiously awaited.

The second narrative accounts for the origin of divinity, which it defines in terms of the king's genealogy, and alludes to the ritual in which humans transform a king into a god.

Narrative 2

Four brothers founded a community. Three contested the ownership of a sacred water jar that their ancestors had carried from their land of origin. The jar broke and the waters that poured out swamped the entire community. Only the fourth brother, until then a marginal figure, was saved. He became the owner of the lagoon, the lord of the water (*we na'in*), a divinized man. Through a ritual of consecration the spirit of the fourth brother would, in later generations, become reincarnated in the person of the king of Balibo. As a reminder of this episode members of each subsequent generation were to be shown a staff that rises vertically from the middle of the lagoon, and which, so informants claim, is the top of the main pillar of an *uma lulik* which stood at the centre of the drowned community. It represents, they add, the axis of the world.

If Narrative 1 explains the origins of the lagoon and the dual character of the social collectivity of Bemalai, Narrative 2 focuses more upon the community's unity and introduces the origin of the notion of man-as-god.

ANALYSIS

The king must die at Bemalai because only he represents the entire society and can therefore mediate the division between humans and spirits, and between society and nature.[20] For ordinary persons, contact with religious forces may, as Hubert and Mauss (1898: 134) claim, be dangerous (Bovensiepen's aforementioned remarks are again apposite); but kings are not ordinary persons – and divine ones presumably even less so. The Tetum term for king, *liurai*, can be literally translated as 'more than the earth', (*liu* [more than] + *rai* [earth]), a gloss that suggests a certain estranged quality in keeping with the king's divine potential. It is also all of a piece with the alien origins some Timorese attribute to kings and their families (cf. Sahlins 1983). At Bemalai, only ritual makes a king divine; as Hubert and Mauss pointed out: '*La victime n'arrive pas nécessairement au sacrifice avec une nature religieuse, achevée et définie; c'est le sacrifice lui-même qui la lui confère*' (1898: 133). The Bemalai victim becomes divine by transcending metaphysical, gender ('The chiefs conjoin [the] two powers' associated with masculinity and femininity [Renard-Clamagirand 1982: 297]), and affinal distinctions,[21] as a consequence of which his death and resurrection are made to correspond to the cyclical reproduction of the society for which he stands.

As encompassing representative of an (albeit temporary) social collectivity, a representative who transcends male and female, sym-

---

20 Since neither the Tetum nor the Ema language apparently has terms for 'society' and 'nature', it might be objected that a contrast between society and nature is merely an analytical contrivance; but it is clear that the ritual and its attendant beliefs implicitly entail this conceptual distinction.

21 Although Feeley-Harnik (1985: 297) has observed that '[o]ne of the most striking features of the literature on divine kingship is the absence of attention to women', we have seen that inflections of the feminine occur frequently in the ritual and accompanying narratives at Bemalai. In narratives, the conflict between the woman and the two men creates two separate communities; the occasion of the ritual is at the beginning of the feminine season; two female beasts are sacrificed; and the ritual is replete with implications of fertility and femininity.

bolizes affinal unity, and provides the counterpart of the local god, the king transcends these contrasts. He is therefore suitably positioned to reconcile them in a n act of creativity set in motion by a ritual that transforms a human being into a spirit controlling fertility and life, and then back again into a human being (Cinatti 1965: 41). By his self-sacrifice, the king is also offering up himself-as-society to the divinity who, revivified by the gift,[22] is thereby afforded the opportunity of reciprocating with the gift of life to both society and nature in what Hocart called a 'communal pursuit of fertility' (1970: 217). By conjoining the spiritual and human orders, the king helps his fellow-spirits and fellow-humans alike, ensuring that both receive life (Cinatti 1965: 41).[23] Furthermore, as oblation and mediator for between human and spiritual and between nature and society, the king-as-divinity serves as a metaphor of the cosmos itself.[24] The ensuing regenerative interaction between spiritual and human is made possible only by the sacrifice of someone who represents the total dually-structured community and has power over the natural resources of the lagoon. Renard-Clamagirand (Clamagirand 1980: 150) has made a point of emphasizing that the Ema associate the *liurai* with the increase of animal resources, adding that 'at the collective level, rituals ... attempt to obtain additional animals from the Liurai who has power over them and is their source'. The connection between rulers and life-sustaining largesse is reinforced by the ritual function

---

22 'The sacrifice ... restores to the spirit ... the sacred energy enjoyed by human beings during the fishing and the commensality that derives from it' (Cinatti 1965: 41).

23 'The object of the ritual is to make the macrocosm bound in the objects of men's desires. But the spirit of the macrocosm resides in the victim, and so prosperity is to be attained by making that microcosm prosperous and bountiful' (Hocart 1970: 202).

24 Cf. Hocart (1970: 69): 'Man *is* not a microcosm; he has to be made one in order that he may control the universe for prosperity. The ritual establishes an equivalence that was not there. If it were there already there would be no point in having a ritual; man would merely have to behave as he wished the world to behave, and there would be no need of words, of altars, and other methods of effecting the identity.'

of another category of Ema leader, the *bei*, who is 'directly responsible for the well-being of the community and who ensures it receives the nourishment it needs' (Renard-Clamagirand 1982: 289).

That ritual serves as a device for integrating smaller units into a larger aggregation among the Ema is at no time more evident than when the rainy season commences:

'It is through [the songs and dances which accompany the arrival of the rains] that the unity of the group is manifested and forged. In effect, these festivals are the occasion on which the ties that unite all the participants are tightened and, as a result, social cohesion is reaffirmed' (Renard-Clamagirand 1982: 289).

CONCLUSION

In calling attention to the sociological approach to divine kingship taken by scholars such as Evans-Pritchard (1948) and Seligman (1934), Vaughan suggests that '[t]he concept of a divine king is the consequence of a world view which holds that the king and his kingdom are one; therefore, prosperity and failings in either must be present in both. Consequently, a king can be held responsible for all conditions in the kingdom. Should he be weak or ill, the kingdom will be in danger; or should the kingdom be in failing circumstances, there must be something wrong with the king. Finally, a change in the person of the king will change the conditions in the kingdom' (1987: 122–23).

As we have seen, while the Bemalai king does indeed symbolize his 'kingdom', he is certainly no ailing symbol of the society he heads. As the dry season draws to a close, it must seem to the people living around the lagoon that it is nature and the divinity of the water that are losing vitality rather than the society's most prominent member. On the contrary, the life-bestowing potency of a surrogate in all the virility of healthy manhood has to be tapped in order to revivify an ailing natural world and divinity, and replenish society with the means of reproducing itself.

In contrast to the Jukun king (Young 1966: 148) and certain other sovereigns described in the literature, whose divinity appears to have endured for their entire lifetimes, the Bemalai king's divinity is short-lived and cyclical. Reanimated in ritual, the king becomes a spirit and is then returned to mortal flesh, thereby permitting the natural world to continue its own cyclical progression into another wet season. In their distinctive way the Timorese appear to be saying that 'the Word' is altogether too remote to help them in their perennial quest for fertility and that mere flesh, even in the guise of a king, lacks sufficient inspiration to generate the resources required. Accordingly, one who is simultaneously both god and king must be conjured up if their quest is to bear fruit. And since the people of Bemalai lagoon have no divine king to call upon, in a ritual performed every few years besides its waters, they must perforce make one.

In his formulation of Hawaiian kingship, Valeri (1985: 344–46) has maintained that communal rituals can be interpreted as a procedure for making participants conscious of their society's basic concepts and principles. But rather than putting themselves in a position of merely 'receiving messages', as Lévi-Strauss (1958) or Leach (1969) might have claimed, ritual allows them to act out the 'only experience they can have of society manifesting itself as unity and multiplicity, that is, of the unity of the species realized as a coordinated complex of social actors' (Valeri 1985: 345). Valeri (Ibid.: 348) concludes that in their rituals Hawaiians introject the complex of links between their image of themselves as a society, the principles that order their society, and the acquisition of land as a source of life. If my interpretation of the *sau-biu* ritual is correct, then it supports Valeri's argument, for the symbols that define the ritual suggest that those who perform it are as concerned with asserting control over natural resources as the Hawaiians and are acting out the same kinds of concepts as those Valeri has identified.

It would therefore seem that by sacrificing their king the people of Bemalai do not only bring land, control over fertility, life, divinity, and kingship into a synthetic unity, but make it also possible for them to sacrifice themselves as a collectivity ('society') by transforming king and society into a god who, revitalized by the sacrifice, reasserts his power to restore life. In performing this, the ultimate act of self-ab-

71

negation, the collectivity impresses upon its members its power to recreate itself as a divinity and hence restore itself to life. In this sense the king is no more divine than the society he represents; but no less divine than the god he becomes.[25]

Their calendrical ritual thus allows the people who convene at the Bemalai lagoon to recreate periodically their society in the image of their god. Like all divinities, their god depends upon human beings for existence, and making their king divine is their way of realizing this god-making capacity. Durkheim understood the concepts of god and society to be related metaphorically, but did not explain how their common identity might, in practice, be conserved in the imaginations of believers or generated in the first place. The ritual analysed here suggests one possible explanation. Society, in the form of a king, becomes divinized by ritual,[26] and since god, originally conceived of and generated in narrative, is recreated every time the ritual is repeated, periodically sacrificing its king is one way by which a society renews its concept of divinity and its own existence as an abstract collectivity.

REFERENCES

Beidelman, T. O. 1966. 'Swazi Royal Ritual'. *Africa* 36: 373–405.

—— 1987. 'Sacrifice and Sacred Rule in Africa'. *American Ethnologist* 14: 542–51.

Bloch, Maurice 1986. *From Blessing to Violence: History and ideology in the circumcision ritual of the Merina of Madagascar.* Cambridge University Press.

---

25 Cf. Galey (1990: 3): 'Neither the divine nor the king are in themselves the ultimate values of society. They are merely expressions of the principles governing its identity. And as we are dealing with relations and not with substances bounded once and for all in a closed set of meaning, the principles may change and the relations be transformed. Thus, to fancy that kingship lives either below or above the limits of society is to misconceive fatally both the nature of kingship and that of society.'

26 Lehmann (1993: 30) has remarked that although 'Durkheim is widely known for his theory that 'God' is really society ... he believed, equally, that society is really God'.

Brandewie, Ernest and Simon Asten. 1976. 'Northern Belunese (Tetum) Marriage and Kinship: A Study of Symbols'. *Philippine Quarterly of Culture and Society* 4: 19–30.

Carlson, R. G. 1993. 'Hierarchy and the Haya divine kingship: A structural and symbolic reformulation of Frazer's Thesis'. *American Ethnologist* 20: 312–35.

Cinatti, Rui 1965. 'A Pescaria da Be-Malai: Mito e Rito'. *Geographica* 1, 32–51.

Clamagirand, Brigitte 1980. 'The Social organization of the Ema of Timor'. In *The Flow of Life: Essays on Eastern Indonesia*, ed. by James J. Fox. Cambridge, MA: Harvard University. Press.

Duarte, Jorge Barros 1964. 'Barlaque'. *Seara* 2, (n. s.) (3): 1–4.

—— n. d. A nascente 'Lulik' de 'Corluli'. Unpublished MS.

Durkheim, E. 1960 (1912) *Les formes élémentaires de la vie religieuse: le système totémique en Australie.* Paris: Presses Universitaires de France.

Evans-Pritchard, E. E. 1948. 'The divine kingship of the Shilluk of the Nilotic Sudan', (Frazer Lecture 1948). Cambridge: University Press. Reprinted in E. E. Evans-
Pritchard *Essays in Social Anthropology*. London: Faber & Faber.

—— 1956. *Nuer Religion*. Oxford: Clarendon Press.

—— 1964. 'Foreword'. In *Sacrifice: Its nature and function* by Henri Hubert and Marcel Mauss (trans.) W.D. Halls. Chicago: University of Chicago Press.

—— 1965. *Theories of Primitive Religion*. Oxford: Clarendon Press.

Feeley-Harnik, G. 1985. 'Issues in Divine Kingship'. *Annual Review of Anthropology*. 14: 273–313.

Fox, James J. 1980. 'Introduction'. In *The Flow of Life: Essays on Eastern Indonesia* (ed.) James J. Fox. Cambridge, MA: Harvard University. Press.

Galey, J.-C. 1990. Introduction. In *Kings and the Kings,* ed. by J.-C. Galey. London: Harwood Academic.

Girard, R. 1992. *Violence and the sacred*. Translated by P. Gregory. Baltimore: Johns Hopkins Press.

Grijzen, H. J. 1904. 'Mededeelingen omtrent Beloe of Midden-Timor'. In Verhandelingen van het Bataviaasch Genootschap van Kunsten en Wetenschappen' 54. Batavia: Albrecht and Co., The Hague: Martinus Nijhoff.

Heusch, L. de. 1985. *Sacrifice in Africa: A structuralist approach*. Transl. by L. O'Brien & A. Morton. Bloomington: Indiana University Press.

—— 1990a. Nkumi et 'Nkumu: la sacralisation du pouvoir chez les Mongo (Zaire)'. In L. de Heusch (ed.) l990b.

—— (ed.) 1990b. *Chefs et rois sacrés: systèmes de pensées en Afrique Noire*. Paris: I.: Ecole Pratique des Hautes Etudes.

Hicks, David 1984. *A Maternal Religion: The role of women in Tetum myth and ritual*. Dekalb: Center for Southeast Asian Studies, Northern Illinois University.

—— 1992. 'Mythos und Ritual: eine Fallstudie aus Timor'. In *Mythen im Kontext: Ethnologische Perspektivetiven*, edited by K-H. Kohl. Frankfurt/Mainz: Qumran im Campus Verlag.

Hocart, Arthur Maurice 1954. *Social Origins*. London: Watts.

—— 1970. *Kings and Councillors: A study in the comparative anatomy of human society*, edited by Rodney Needham. Chicago: University of Chicago Press.

Hubert, Henri and Marcel Mauss 1898. 'Essai sur la nature et la function du Sacrifice'. *Année Sociologique* 2: 29–138.

King, Margret 1963. *Eden to Paradise*. London: Hodder & Stoughton.

—— 1965. 'Fishing Rites at Be-Malai, Portuguese Timor'. *Records of the South Australian Museum*. 15: 109–17.

Leach, Edmund 1969. *Genesis as Myth and Other Essays*. London: Cape.

Lehmann, J. M. 1993. *Deconstructing Durkheim: A post post structuralist critique*. New York: Routledge.

Lévi-Strauss, Claude 1958. *Anthropologie structurale*. Paris: Pion.

Lukes, S. 1985. *Emile Durkheim: His life and work; a critical and historical study.*

Stanford: Stanford University Press.

Muller, J.-C. 1980. *Le roi bouc émissaire: pouvoirs et rituels chez les Rukuba du Nigéria central.* Paris: L'Harmattan.

Needham, Rodney 1980. *Reconnaissances.* Toronto: University Press.

Pascoal, Ezequiel Enes 1967. *A Alma de Timor Vista Na Sua Fantasia: lendas, fábula e contos.* Braga: Barbosa & Xavier, Lda.

Renard-Clamagirand, Brigitte 1987. *Marobo: Une Société Ema de Timor.* Paris: Center National de la Recherche Scientifique.

Richards, Audrey I. 1969. 'Keeping the King Divine'. *Proceedings of the Royal Anthropological Institute 1968*, 23–35.

Sahlins, Marshall 1983. 'Raw Women, Cooked Men, and Other "Great things" of the Fiji Islands'. In *The Ethnography of Cannibalism*, edited by Paula Brown and Donald Tuzin. Washington, DC: Society for Psychological Anthropology.

Seligman, C. G. 1934. *Egypt and Negro Africa.* London: G. Routledge & Sons.

Valeri, Valerio 1985. *Kingship and Sacrifice: Ritual and society in ancient Hawaii* translated by P. Wissing. Chicago: University of Chicago Press.

Vaughan, J. H. 1987. 'A Reconsideration of Divine Kingship'. In *Explorations in African Systems of Thought*, edited by Ivan Karp and C. S. Bird. Bloomington: Indiana University Press.

Vondra, J. G. 1968. *Timor journey.* Wellington/Auckland: A. H. & A. W. Reed.

Vroklage, B. A. C. 1952. *Ethnographie der Belu in Zentral-Timor.* Leiden: E.J. Brill.

Wortelboer, W. 1952. *Monotheisme bij de Belu's op Timor? Anthropos* 47: 290–92.

Young, M. W. 1966. 'The Divine Kingship of the Jukun: A re-evaluation of some theories'. *Africa* 36: 135–53.

CHAPTER 5

Divine Kings and
Younger Brothers

his chapter[1] concerns the relationship between secular (or material) and spiritual modes of being[2] as they
relate to an instance of what might be referred to as
'divine kingship' among a community of Timorese residing in
two villages, Balibo and Atabae, which lie near a lagoon on the
northern shores of central Timor.[3] We should note that the term
'divine king' is open to criticism on the grounds that it does not
denote a monothetic class of sovereign at all, and as employed
cross-culturally has come to include diverse congeries of political and religious practitioners who have little in common apart
from being connected in variable ways with spiritual entities
themselves often highly variegated in character. Gillian Feeley-
Harnik's conspectus (1985), the article by Michael W. Young
(1966: 135–36), and the collection of papers edited by Young
(1966: 135–36), each attest to the culture-bound constitution
of this designation and give one ample cause to be wary about
using it. All the same, although there may be analytic benefits

---

1   In its original form the substance of this chapter appeared in a paper dedi-
cated to Clark Cunningham (Hicks 1998) and I take pleasure in reaffirming
my dedication. An autobiographical note by way of reminiscence might not
be amiss. I was first prompted into carrying out fieldwork in Timor after
attending Cunningham's seminar on the Atoni diarchy given during one
of the Friday weekly seminar series at the Institute of Social Anthropology
at the University of Oxford in 1962 or 1963. I am grateful to the Wenner-
Gren Foundation for Anthropological Research for making it possible for
me to carry out research in Lisbon. I also thank Lorraine Aragon, Jennifer
Callans, and Susan Russell for helpful criticisms.
2   Endicott (1970: 96) has identified a somewhat similar distinction (i.e.,
'between body and essence') in Malay thought.
3   See Chapter 4.

to be gained from the use of a more generalizing term such as 'sacred leader' or 'sacred chief', this is not the occasion for arguing for an alternative designation; so, for the purposes of the present chapter, I shall follow conventional usage. To my knowledge, the term has not been applied within the context of any Timorese population except the one to be discussed here, and it may be that this society is unique in possessing a figure that may be thus designated.

Portugal began its presence on Timor in the 16th century, and during the succeeding 350 years gradually consolidated its position in the eastern sector of Timor and a small enclave along the northern shores of western Timor. In September 1975, a breakdown of colonial control in this bifurcated territory resulted in a civil war between Timorese political factions. The victorious faction, called Fretilin, declared 'East Timor' an independent nation, but the armies of the Republic of Indonesia invaded the country on 7 December 1975 and quickly overcame the military opposition that they faced and remained in illegal occupation until 1999.

The villagers of Balibo speak Tetum; those of Atabae speak Ema. Bemalai lagoon is a stretch of water rich in fish and crustaceans that are preyed upon by crocodiles. Until the late 1960s, at least, members of both villages would gather together every few years to perform a ritual in which a local king would be symbolically sacrificed to the divinity of the waters. After this, he would be restored to life.

The divinity in question is a member of a class of elementals known as *we na'in* (lords of the water). These spirits may be considered refractions of a deity identified as an earth goddess and are credited with powers both beneficent and malign (Grijzen 1904: 74–77). These divine refractions confer wealth and fertility on those who offer them sacrifices. Persons who refrain or neglect to do so, on the other hand, may expect to become afflicted by sickness, infertility or death. When they establish relationships with human beings these spirits incarnate themselves as aquatic creatures – typically sharks, turtles, or eels; but perhaps their most typical manifestation is in the form of a crocodile, a creature believed to be ancestrally related to certain descent groups.

A RITUAL OF KINGS

This chapter considers a pair of narratives that relate to this royal ritual. As I argued in Chapter 4, by offering his life in this ritual of regicide, a local king is transformed into both society and god, and the activities involved in the ritual coming together of the participants for the purpose of changing the ontological status of their king constitutes a strategy by which two local communities of the Tetum and Ema periodically regenerate indigenous notions of 'society' and 'god' as epistemological categories. During the performance of the ritual, certain narratives are recited by an official story-teller known as the *lia na' in* or 'lord of the word'. In Chapter 4 we saw that they are integral components of the ritual performance itself – a connection explicitly made by two principal sources for the ritual, Cinatti (1965) and King (1965), who include them in their respective descriptions. There exist, however, two other narratives that have a bearing on the ritual, and their relevance for it has yet to be remarked. One purpose of this chapter, therefore, is to show how these narratives contribute to the meaning of the ritual.

My second intention is to reveal connections – hitherto unrecorded so far as I am aware – between local notions of divine kingship and the kinship figure of the younger brother. The conclusions that I shall offer relate exclusively to the ethnically mixed Bemalai population, but a comparative ethnography of Timorese cultures suggests that they might have a much wider applicability on the island.

The Portuguese text of the first narrative was provided – and generously placed at my disposal in 1989 – by Father Jorge Barros Duarte (Duarte n. d.) who had heard it from the sexton of the Church of Motael in Dili, a man called Francisco, sometime in 1962. The following is a free translation of this hitherto unpublished document.

The initial phoneme *cor* in the title, which appears in the original manuscript, might, according to Father Duarte, be a personal name.

Narrative 1. The Sacred Spring of Corluli

The spring known as Corluli is sacred (*lulik*). From it originates the lagoon of Bemalai, according to the residents of Maliana Plain, where it is situated. The full name of Corluli spring is Corluli Bau-Soe, which means 'the bubbling spring of the good-natured Bau'. Locals tell the following narrative.

An old man called Bau had three children. These were a girl and two boys. The girl was called Olo-Mau. I do not know the names of the brothers. The elder brother worked on the land. One day, the younger brother took a fishing hook from his elder brother, and went to fish at Corluli. He caught a crocodile that ripped the hook from the fishing line; it got stuck in the creature's throat.

When the younger brother returned home, his elder brother inquired about the hook, so the former explained how it had come to be lost in the crocodile's mouth. The elder brother refused to believe him and demanded compensation.

The younger brother grew betel and decided to attend to his crop (perhaps to get out of his elder brother's way). Upon his arrival, he discovered that some of his leaves had been stolen. Six times he returned to the place where his crop was, and each time always with the same result. On the last occasion, however, he spotted a white cockatoo in the creepers. Here was the thief! What he did not know was that the bird was actually a woman. He asked the bird why it had stolen his leaves. The cockatoo replied: 'I came to collect these betel leaves to cure the wound of grandfather (*emu*).' The lad asked: 'What sort of wound?' The cockatoo explained that the wound was in the throat. The younger brother said: 'I think I could cure your grandfather's wound.' 'Then come with me', the bird said, 'Let's go and cure him.' The young man cut a piece of palm leaf with the spines attached and concealed it in a fold in his sarong. When they were ready to depart he asked the cockatoo: 'Where must we go?'

'Close your eyes!' she ordered. He did as he was told, and then instantly opened them again to find himself in her house, where he saw the ailing grandfather stretched out on the ground. 'What's the matter?' asked the lad. The grandfather replied: 'I have been ill for seven days.' The young man ordered the assembled onlookers to leave, then told the grandfather to close his eyes. The younger brother extracted the hook, swiftly concealing it in a fold of his sarong. When the crocodile opened his eyes, the lad showed him – instead of the hook – the piece of palm leaf that he had secreted away. He told the crocodile that it was this that had made his throat sick. Seeing himself cured, the crocodile asked his benefactor what reward he desired – money, a pretty woman, anything else he might wish for. The young man wanted only buffaloes. The crocodile instructed him to build a corral. When the lad had done so, the crocodile ordered him to close and open his eyes seven times. Each time when he closed and opened them, the buffaloes increased in number until they completely filled the corral.

The crocodile then asked the young man for a woman to serve him. The young man offered him a slave. The crocodile refused. He wanted a princess of the same blood as the younger brother. The lad brought the crocodile his own sister. This was Olo-mau, who had remained at home, but who now married the crocodile.

Every year, at the time of the first rains [about November], a great ritual is carried out at the sacred spring of Corluli to beg a blessing of rain from the grandfather.[4] For this ritual it is necessary to sacrifice a female buffalo and a female pig, both of the colour red, and to use a sacred spear which must be thrust through the vagina of the buffalo. The pig is killed and its entrails tied up into a bundle. The meat of both animals, together with some rice, has to remain exposed on the banks of the sacred spring for the grandfather to eat.

The plot opens in the human domain where the 'no nonsense' elder brother works at providing food for the household while the younger

---

4   I.e., the Bemalai ritual.

brother undertakes the pleasant but less demanding and reliable activity of fishing. Despite this contrast, both brothers occupy themselves carrying out the mundane tasks of everyday life that humans must perform. This normal, settled pattern of life comes to an end when a shape-shifting female creature breaks into the human world. The miraculous being possesses the power of enabling a normal human being to emulate her and enter the other world – in this case by closing his eyes. The denizens of this fabulous subaquatic realm are lords of the water incarnated as crocodiles, one of which is referred to, in human terms, as 'grandfather'. He, too, commands supra-normal powers and later empowers the younger brother with the ability to miraculously provision himself with buffaloes. The young man reciprocates by giving his sister to the crocodile, thereby forming an affinal relationship with himself having precedence as wife-giver. The affinal ties linking them are subsequently reaffirmed in the annual ritual sacrifice of a female buffalo and female pig, presumably to induce the crocodile to bring rain at the proper time.

The narrative describes how a fruitful relationship between a human male and a female elemental is forged by the exchange of presents,[5] that is, an increase in animal resources (fertility) in exchange for women (fertility), and how it is maintained by the exchange of rainfall (and the fertility enhancing qualities that it confers) for the sacrifice of a female buffalo and a female pig.

Various stock features of Timorese younger brother tales appear in this story: (1) a journey to the spirit domain; (2) a curative method entailing deception; (3) the hero's wily nature; (4) the hostile relationship with the elder brother that precipitates the younger brother's journey; and (5) a series of antitheses by means of which this relationship is defined.[6] The younger brother embarks on an incredible journey; the elder brother remains at home, presumably

---

5 Comparable to the exchange of bride and bridewealth between wife-givers and wife-takers in the *fetosa-umane*.

6 Mention, too, might be made of the fishing hook, a motif occurring in a number of Timorese tales as well as on other islands in eastern Indonesia (see Chapters 6, 7 and 8.

continuing in the quotidian and subsistence occupation of a farmer. The younger brother demonstrates craftiness and is quick-witted; in failing to believe the truth when he hears it, the elder brother appears as somewhat obtuse. The younger brother's 'hook' is a natural product; the elder brother's hook is an artefact of culture. Finally, the younger brother amasses a new resource, a herd of buffaloes; the elder brother forfeits his customary resource, his hook.

The missionary, Ezequiel Enes Pascoal (1967: 132–37), acquired the second narrative from a teacher of the Catholic Catechism, Isaac dos Reis, who for many years was a resident of Balibo. Another man, called 'Evaristo', who lived in Ro-Mean, in Manu-Sa'e, in the region of Hatolia, confirmed it. Evaristo, though baptized, Pascoal notes, lived a 'fully pagan life', and was one of the most learned local men in traditions and legends. The following is a free translation. As with the previous narrative, I have retained its original title.

Narrative 2. Bemalai

Loho-Rai – a native of Behali (or Wehali, a kingdom on the south central coast of Timor) – whose wife was Nona-Bika, daughter of the king of Cava (a region to the east of Wehali), installed himself in the region where today one finds Bemalai. He had seven children. Six occupied themselves by labouring in their gardens, but Bili-Loba, the youngest brother, heedless of his parents' wishes, preferred hunting. Every evening, to appear like his elder brothers, he would deliberately dirty himself and his machete with soil, implying he had worked beside them. Then one day, either because his parents suspected him or because his brothers denounced him, his father visited the garden to make sure that Bili-Loba was working. Failing to find him with his brothers, the father hid in a thicket in the forest, from which vantage point he spotted his youngest son hunting. That night his mother punished the lad by putting excrement beneath the food on his plate. When Bili-Loba discovered it, he cried out in fury and went to live by himself in Kilibai, which lies at the foot of Mount Samono[7] which rises above

7 This mountain is about 5 kilometres southeast of the lagoon.

Bemalai. The young man had no choice but to make himself a garden. Because there was plenty of water he chose to cultivate areca and betel. Eventually he married.

After marrying, Bili-Loba began fishing in the sea. One day his hook caught a fish of uncommon weight. He tried pulling it towards land but his line broke. Bili-Loba returned home feeling too wretched to sleep. He had lost his 'daily bread' and could not obtain a new hook quickly. An even greater misfortune befell him when in the morning he saw that someone had stolen his areca and betel.

The following night he lay in watch for the thief. No one came. Only a cockatoo which, arriving at dawn, settled down in an areca tree and transformed himself – to the considerable astonishment of the watcher – into a man. Convinced that he was unobserved, the stranger helped himself to as much areca and betel as he wished. Cautiously Bili-Loba approached as closely as possible, until he was near enough to confront the thief. He demanded that the man come down from the tree immediately. If he disobeyed, said Bili-Loba, he would shoot an arrow through him. The man descended and Bili-Loba demanded payment: 'Don't leave before you pay me for the areca and betel you have stolen.'

Gripped tightly by Bili-Loba and seeing that he could not get away, the thief replied: 'I didn't steal for myself. I stole for the queen who is seriously wounded and needs the areca and betel to be cured.'

'Liar! If you do not pay me you will not leave this place!'

'If you don't believe me, come with me to the queen's house!' replied the man.

Bili-Loba agreed to go, but kept the man prisoner. Together they set out for the beach. When they arrived, the thief said: 'Close your eyes!'

Bili-Loba closed them. Moments later, the thief said to him: 'Open them!'

Opening his eyes, Bili-Loba saw that he was in the house of a queen who was surrounded by people who had come with medicines to cure her, but to no avail. Bili-Loba was asked if he had something with which to ameliorate her suffering. As he came near the invalid, he noticed that she had a hook caught in her throat – the self-same hook that he had lost in the sea two days before. Intent on restoring her health, Bili-Loba proclaimed confidently: 'I have a cure for the queen. I am just going outside to look for the remedy and will return without delay.'

When he returned he requested that everyone leave him alone with his patient. Otherwise, he said, there would be no cure. Free from the gaze of curious eyes, Bili-Loba pulled out the hook so adroitly that the queen never noticed exactly what he did. Then, for her benefit, he produced a thorn that he had extracted from a palm tree in the forest. 'Here's what was making your throat so painful your majesty.' Soon the queen felt so good she was able to speak and eat and the first thing she said was to tell Bili-Loba that she would repay him with whatever he asked for. The king, for his part, did not wait for Bili-Loba to make a request. He immediately ordered rice and milk for him.

Bili-Loba had not drunk milk since he was a child, and enjoyed it greatly. Seeing his pleasure, the king and queen said: 'Return to Kilibai. There make seven corrals, each of gradually increasing size, with the seventh the biggest.'

Well satisfied with the result of his adventure, Bili-Loba suddenly found himself on the beach by the same marvellous process that had transported him to the palace. From the beach he travelled to Kilibai, where he worked hard at constructing the seven corrals. After he had finished, he again walked to the beach to talk with the king. The same man who had robbed him of areca and betel was there waiting. Again he told him to close and open his eyes. Bili-Loba did so. In an instant Bili-Loba found himself before the king and queen, who said: 'Now that you have made the corrals, return to Kilibai. Make two large baskets with the leaves of a lontar palm. Fill one with beans and leave the other empty. Before dawn place one to the right and the other to the left of the entrance to the first corral. Like the other six, this must remain open. Buffaloes too plentiful to count will soon appear. Each time a beast enters the corral, toss a bean from the full basket into the empty basket. When the supply of beans is exhausted so, too, will be the supply of buffaloes.'

Returning to Kilibai, Bili-Loba spent the night carrying out the royal instructions. At dawn he heard a tremendous noise in the distance. It grew closer and closer, increasing like a tempest from the sea and shaking the palm trees wildly. The buffaloes! One by one, without anyone guiding them, they entered the corrals. They kept entering for hours. There were indeed as many as the number of beans that Bili-Loba was emptying out of the basket. When only a single bean remained, the largest of all the buffaloes entered the seventh corral. He was so huge that his long horns grazed the entrance with a terrific rumble, causing all seven corrals to tremble. The gates closed by themselves.

Bili-Loba's wife and their maid, who was called Bau, then gathered up the baskets and the beans. These objects were henceforth classed as *lulik*. In all the region no one was as rich as Bili-Loba.

Learning of Bili-Loba's wealth, his brothers visited him. Claiming that as elder brothers they were entitled to the buffaloes, they forced him to surrender the entire herd, and ignoring his strenuous protests, they took the beasts away with them.

Bili-Loba decided to complain to his benefactors. So he went to the beach. By opening and closing his eyes, and with the help of the same man, he once more found himself in the palace. Learning about the extortion the king said: 'Go build an outrigger. When you have finished hide the boat from everyone's sight and come and tell me.'

He did as instructed and observed every precaution so no one might know what he was doing. Bili-Loba then found his helper and, closing and opening his eyes, reported to the king. He did not return home straight away, however, as he had done before because the king had instructed him to visit Corluli-Bau-Sai [probably a variation of 'Bau-soe' in the first tale], the sacred spring of Maliana. The following day Bili-Loba travelled as part of the retinue of the queen who was going to visit her elder son, a young prince who resided there.

As dawn lit the sky the travellers were already on the beach. There, all of them except for Bili-Loba, transformed themselves into crocodiles and entered the water. Bili-Loba had to be carried by a crocodile orderly of the crocodile queen.[8]

Arriving at the River Loes,[9] the party climbed out of the water and continued on to the River Bebai to reach its confluence with the waters from Corluli-Bau-Sai Spring. From here Bili-Loba saw in the far distance the little figure of the queen's first-born son.

The queen said to Bili-Loba: 'Now that you have seen my son go right away and fetch Kolo, your daughter.[10] I wish them to marry.'

Detecting a hint of uneasiness in his countenance and fearing a deception of some kind, the queen warned Bili-Loba: 'If the young woman you bring is truly your daughter, the Corluli waters will recognize her and throw up high spumes. But should it not be her the waters will continue to flow normally.'

As usual, closing and opening his eyes brought Bili-Loba to Kilibai. He related the queen's demand to Nona Bika, Kolo's mother. She was indignant, finding such a marriage displeasing. Her arguments convinced Bili-Loba that their maid, Bau, would have to be given in place of his daughter. She would sparkle resplendently in silver and gold earrings and bracelets. Hanging down from her neck and criss-crossing her breasts would be expensive and gorgeous coral necklaces. Her black, ebony-like hair would be embellished by combs embroidered with silver. Her sarong, which would reach up to enclose her breasts, would be woven by the most talented weavers available. Seeing her thus, thought Nona Bika, even the waters of Corluli-Bau-sai would be fooled.

---

8   Probably on the animal's back – the customary manner of conveyance in such tales (Hicks 1988: 807).

9   A river 6 kilometres north of Atabae.

10 The name 'Kolo' may be a variant of Olo-[Mau], the sister in the first narrative, since both women serve as mediators between the spiritual and material domains.

Received with pleasure by the queen and her entourage, Bau scooped water from the spring. The flow of water continued unabated, fresh and clear, without the ripple of a single curl of spume. The queen scolded Bili-Loba for his attempt to deceive them: 'Return, and if you do not bring your daughter, Kolo, your complaint against your brothers will be ignored!'

This time, despite his wife's objections, Bili-Loba offered his daughter, Kolo, who was so magnificently adorned and enveloped in clothing of splendid distinction that neither the queen nor her retainers had ever seen the like. The queen's eldest son, the prince, went with Kolo to the spring, where, as soon as she touched the water the pair disappeared in the highest plumes of spray. No one could see them.

'Now you will be able to avenge yourself against your brothers', said the queen. 'Take this gourd. It is full of water endowed with a strange power.'

Respectfully, Bili-Loba took the vessel and carried it to his brothers' hamlet. When he reached Kutubaba, he stumbled in the immense *lulik* grassland of Damlara [Damelaran] and in a trice a vast lagoon spread from the spot where a single drop of water had been spilt from the gourd.

Bili-Loba's brothers were surprised when he arrived, a surprise which was all the greater when, upon showing them the water in the gourd, Bili-Loba said: 'Henceforth, not even at the height of the dry season will you lack water! There will appear a great and strange spring that will never dry up. But first the community must hold a festival in which everyone must participate. Celebrations will continue for several days.'

The brothers ordered all the drums of the region beaten and every horn blown. They invited everyone and assembled them together for the festival to prepare for the advent of the remarkable spring. The festival was scheduled to last seven days and seven nights.

That first night the local men and women danced with furious animation in great circles to the rhythm of their songs that echoed loudly across the land. If the enthusiasm slackened somewhat

88

during the day, it was only to increase the following night. The abundance of meat and wine helped keep the orgy at a peak – which was exactly what Bili-Loba wanted, because only if the revellers were preoccupied would it be possible for him to retrieve the hidden outrigger. His brothers' carefree drinking aided him in the execution of his plan.

At the festival's culmination on the seventh night, Bili-Loba erected a pillar at the centre of the community's *uma lulik* and fastened a length of wood to it at right angles. On one side of this horizontal bar he attached the gourd containing the water from Corluli-Bau-sai. On the other side he attached bones of slaughtered buffaloes [probably slaughtered during the festival]. As Bili-Loba had foreseen, the dogs from the hamlet came and attacked the bones. They fought furiously among themselves for possession, making a tremendous din all the while. During the *melêe*, the gourd fell onto the floor, spilling all the water as it did so. The earth quivered in a tremendous explosion that blew open a wide vent. Tremendous waves from the sea rushed into it.

Before the earth opened, Bili-Loba had jumped into the outrigger with his wife and his brother, Ika-Bi, the only sibling who had never hurt anyone. The turbulent sea drowned thousands. Only a few persons found safety in Balibo and Atabae. Bili-Loba steered his outrigger towards the River Loes. From there he travelled overland to Vatu-Boro, and later to Guguleur, which is in the land of Maubara, before finally establishing himself in Adi-Goa, Nu'u-Laran. Because he had given his daughter to the queen's first-born child, he acquired another name, that of 'Loro-Kakateu' [sun-cockatoo].[11] From his children, Kari-Mau and Leto-Mau, descended the inhabitants of Manu-Sa'e, in Hatoli. For them this tale is, and will perhaps continue to be for a long time, the most truthful of histories.

---

11 *Loro* is an honorific applied to persons of royal standing and in some Timorese traditions kings are thought to have originated in the spiritual world. Here, after engaging with the strange lords of the water in the realm of spirit, the younger brother is being associated with kingship.

Parallels between the two narratives are readily apparent. In both, a fishing hook snags the mouth of an aquatic creature and is lost. The implement is lost by a younger brother who has an antagonistic relationship with his elder brother or brothers. Estranged, he quits his natal locale and embarks on a venture into the unknown. As though to underscore his marginal status, he is portrayed as cultivating betel (and in this second tale, areca) and fishing instead of growing subsistence crops like his brothers. Yet it is he who eventually attains wealth and power in a reversal of precedence that comes about because he is marginal to the commonplace world where his elders outrank him: he has the power to establish a relationship with the spirit world. In both tales, closing and opening his eyes at the prompting of an emissary transports the younger brother to that mysterious world. Once there, he cures a divine-like crocodile (a female here) and conceals his precise *modus operandi* from his host by a deceptive ploy, substituting a harmless natural 'hook' for the crippling hook that has a cultural source. For his pains, as in the first narrative, he is rewarded with bounty, in this instance seven incrementally augmenting corrals of buffaloes.

At this point the second plot diverges from that of the preceding narrative. First, the elder brothers seize the younger brother's wealth. Next, the spirits transform themselves into their zoological *personae*, one of which transports the younger brother to the sacred spring near which the king and queen's eldest son lives. The prince takes the younger brother's daughter as his wife, thus repeating the establishment of the affinal relationship between human beings and spirits described in the first tale. In both narratives the crocodile's wife mediates between the domains of spirit and matter, like the younger brother (Hicks 1984).

Reprisals against the thieving elder brothers and redress for the victimized younger brother are now in order; it is at this point that the narrative converges with the other two narratives by introducing an incident involving a lethal flood, although here the vessel rent in pieces is not a water jar (as in the other narratives) but a gourd; and it is not two men but dogs that are responsible for its destruction (Hicks 1996).

THE YOUNGER BROTHER

In an earlier paper (Hicks 1988) I argued that in certain Timorese populations the younger brother serves as mediator between two polarized conceptions of experience. Around one pole are grouped imaginative ideas outside the limits of human experience. Around the opposite pole cluster ideas derived from quotidian life. The former pole is variously identified in narratives as located underground, across the sea, over a river, or on top of a mountain. It is a strange and alien domain, the dwelling-place of the spirits. For the Tetum and Ema this world is both the source of life and the destination to which souls of the dead travel after death (Hicks 1988: 807; Renard-Clamagirand 1982: 293). A concomitant metaphysical notion is that human existence can be represented as an oscillation, or cycle, between these poles (Hicks 1988: 809).[12] One expression of these ideas in narrative, as we have seen, employs the motif of a hero who, finding himself marginalized by some incident, undertakes a journey through or over water into the world of the spirits. This man is most commonly a younger brother who eventually returns, now endowed with precedence.

CONCLUSION

In other genre of narrative, too, the role of mediator between matter and spirit devolves upon the younger brother. The origin narratives of descent groups are a case in point. In one Tetum narrative that I collected in Caraubalo *suku* a younger brother is transformed into an eel, a visitor from the world of the spirit, and founds a descent group (*ahi matan*) henceforth known as 'Eel' (Hicks 1984: 24–27): his socially ambivalent, marginalized character accords with this function. In these two Bemalai narratives the younger brother appears in a novel perspective. Although our sources are unclear about whether or not these narratives, unlike the other two narratives associated with Bemalai, are actually recited by the local lord of the word during

---

12 Cf. Barnes's 'spiritual essence' among the Kedang of Lembata (1974: 306–7).

the performance of the ritual,[13] each accords with the ritual. At the same time the overt similarities accumulate only near the end of the two narratives, after a long recital of the younger brother's adventures that would seem to have only tangential connection to the ritual, so it is puzzling why the narrative should go to such lengths to describe them.

One possibility comes to mind in comparing the plots of the narratives with the ritual. In the ritual, a local chief (a king) of Bemalai is ritually put to death to revivify the ailing spirit of the waters of the Bemalai lagoon. Revitalized, the divinity makes the onset of the rainy season and a resurgence of the lagoon's aquatic life possible. As a consequence of the mutually beneficial reciprocity initiated between humanity and divinity, the fertility of both land and water is brought about by the power of divinity. Thus is human life secured in a nexus of reciprocity wrought and maintained by the king's sacrificing himself to resuscitate a debilitated aquatic divinity before being ritually restored to life.

In the narratives a younger brother leaves the material world to cure a debilitated incarnated elemental and returns to the human world to enjoy a more elevated status than his community's *lisan* had hitherto granted him. So close is the resemblance that I would suggest that in this instance at least Edmund Leach's (1954: 13–14) hyperbolic assertion that 'myth regarded as a statement in words 'says' the same thing as ritual regarded as a statement in action' is borne out. In their different modes, the Bemalai ritual and its narratives describe the cyclical nature of existence and the reciprocal ties between human beings and their divinities.[14] Each requires a human sacrifice if the ailing divinity is to be revivified and if the fruits of that divinity's powers are to be bestowed on humanity.

---

13 In one of our conversations, Father Duarte (if I remember correctly) informed me that his text was indeed recited as part of the ritual. It was he who first alerted me to the connection between this tale and the ritual.

14 For an alternative interpretation of the relationship between the Bemalai ritual and its narratives, see Hicks (1992).

But what of the fact that in neither narrative does the younger brother die – ritually or otherwise? Is it not inappropriate to cast him in the role of a sacrificial figure? Here a ritual action analogous to the narrative suggests the answer: the Bemalai king's 'death' is symbolized by the closing of his eyes while his return to 'life' is symbolized by his opening them.

I suggest that the Bemalai ritual and its associated narratives are media for conveying truths of a metaphysical character. The former provides a theatrical forum and the narratives furnish a literary forum for ideas concerning the nature of human existence. The younger brother's literary adventures are homologous with the performative role of the king and so it would appear that for the community of Bemalai the divine king and younger brother are cast as homologous representations. Both 'die', both mediate between the world of the spirit and the world of the flesh, both restore life to an ailing divinity, both bring back life-enhancing abundance, and both transcend death and life. Like the king of Bemalai, the younger brother is endowed with qualities of divinity, an aspect of his character that goes some way to explaining why the aforementioned narrative I heard in Caraubalo[15] ascribes to him the role of divine founder (totem or culture hero) of a clan (Hicks 1984: 24–27).

REFERENCES

Barnes, R. H. 1974. *The Kedang: A Study of the Collective Thought of an Eastern Indonesian People*. Oxford: Clarendon Press.

Cinatti, Rui. 1965. 'A Pescaria da Be-Malai: Mito e Rito'. *Geographica* 1: 32–51.

Cunningham, Clark. 1965. 'Order and Change in an Atoni Diarchy'. *Bijdragen tot de Taal-, Land- en Volkenkunde* 121: 359–82.

Duarte, Jorge Barros. n. d. A Nascente 'Lulik' de 'Corluli'. Unpublished manuscript.

Endicott, Kirk. 1970. *An Analysis of Malay Magic*. Oxford: Clarendon Press.

15 See Chapter 8.

Feeley-Harnik, Gillian. 1985. 'Issues in Divine Kingship'. *Annual Review of Anthropology* 14: 273–313.

Grijzen, H. J. 1904. 'Mededeelingen omtrent Beloe of Midden-Timor'. *Verhandelingen van het Bataviaasch Genootschap van Kunsten en Wetenschappen* 54. Batavia: Albrecht and Co., The Hague: Martinus Nijhoff.

Hicks, David. 1984. *A Maternal Religion: The Role of Women in Tetum Myth and Ritual*. DeKalb: Northern Illinois University, Center for Southeast Asian Studies.

—— 1988. 'Literary Masks and Metaphysical Truths: Intimations from Timor'. *American Anthropologist* 90(4): 807–17.

—— 1992. 'Mythos und Ritual: Eine Fallstudie aus Timor'. In *Mythen im Kontext: Ethnologische Perspektiven*, edited by Karl-Heinz Kohl, pp. 49–78. Frankfurt/Mainz: Qumran im Campus Verlag.

—— 1996. 'Making the King Divine: A Case Study in Ritual Regicide from Timor'. *Journal of the Royal Anthropological Institute* (n. s.) 2: 611–24

—— 1998. 'Divine Kings and Younger Brothers on Timor'. In *Structuralism's Transformations: Order and Revisions in Indonesian and Malaysian Societies*, edited by Lorraine V. Aragon and Susan Russell, pp. 95–113. Tempe, Arizona: Arizona State University.

King, Margaret. 1965. 'Fishing Rites at Be-Malai, Portuguese Timor'. *Records of the South Australian Museum* 15: 109–117.

Leach, Edmund R. 1954. *Political Systems of Highland Burma: A Study of Kachin Social Structure*. London: University of London. School of Economics and Political Science, G. Bell and Sons, Ltd.

Pascoal, Ezequiel Enes. 1967. *A Alma de Timor: Vista na sua Fantasia*. Braga, Portugal: Barbosa & Xavier, LDA.

Renard-Clamagirand, Brigitte. 1982. *Marobo: Une Société Ema de Timor*. Paris: Centre National de la Recherche Scientifique.

Young, Michael W. 1966. 'The Divine Kingship of the Jukun. A Re-Evaluation of Some Theories'. *Africa* 36: 135–53.

CHAPTER 6

Younger Brother and Fishing Hook on Timor

Re-Assessing Mauss on Hierarchy and Divinity

I n two of his most influential essays Marcel Mauss proposes contradictory perspectives on the status relationship between gods
and human beings.[1] In the earlier study, written in collaboration
with his *Année sociologique* colleague Henri Hubert (Hubert and
Mauss 1888), he emphatically asserts the importance of the gifts that
human beings give in ritual sacrifices to the gods.

> *'C'est par le semblable qu'on nourrit le semblable et la victime est la
> nourriture des dieux. Aussi le sacrifice a-t-il été rapidement considéré
> comme la condition même de l'existence divine. C'est lui qui fournit
> la matière immortelle dont vivent les dieux. Ainsi, non seulement c'est
> dans le sacrifice que quelques dieux prennent naissance, mais encore
> c'est par le sacrifice que tous entretiennent leur existence. Il a donc fini
> par apparaître comme leur essence, leur origine, leur créateur'* (Hubert
> and Mauss 1888: 130).[2]

---

1   My thanks go to Professor Gregory Forth and the late Professor Rodney
    Needham for bringing to my attention certain references in the literature
    to the fishing hook motif. I also thank *lia na'in* Domingos Soares, of Uma
    Ua'in Craik *suku*, Viqueque, and *lia na'in* Lequi Rubik, of Caraubalo *suku*,
    Viqueque, for sharing their knowledge of traditional oral literature with me
    during my fieldwork in East Timor in 2005, and the former especially, for
    informing me of the part that the 'lord of the word' plays in Uma Ua'in Craik
    ritual life. I also express gratitude to the Fulbright Committee for selecting
    me for a Fulbright award from the J. William Fulbright Foreign Scholarship
    Board, the Wenner-Gren Foundation for Anthropological Research, and
    the American Philosophical Society for at different times sponsoring my
    Timorese research. Finally, though not least, my thanks to the anonymous
    reviewers of an earlier version of this chapter when it was being considered
    for publication by the Journal of the Royal Anthropological Institute.
2   'Like is fed to like, and the victim is the food of the gods. Thus sacrifice
    quickly came to be considered as the very condition of the divine existence.

The collaborators incorporate into their argument the proposition that the relationship between gods and humans is both contractual in nature and mutually beneficial. If the value of the gifts (food and drink) that the gods receive may appear somewhat paltry in comparison to the value of the gifts (health, fertility, and life) that human beings receive, both prestations are nevertheless equally essential to both partners. Recently, Lygia Sigaud (2002: 337–38) has drawn attention to the fact that Mauss's ideas on what has come to be known as the 'theory' of gift-giving developed over a number of years and it would appear that he was introduced to Boas's material on the Kwakiutl by Durkheim some time before 1905, the year he taught a course at the École Pratique des Hautes Études on the family among the populations of the Northwest Coast. Mauss's ideas about the hierarchical nature of gift-giving are likely to have been influenced by the Northwest Coast data and incorporated into his thinking about exchange over the next two decades, and this may account for the fact that a quarter of a century after his joint paper with Hubert, in the even more influential 'Essai sur le don', he posited a very different opinion, one that depreciated the value of the human prestations, and by corollary diminished the standing of human beings in relation to the divine. His view that 'ces dieux qui donnent et rendent son là pour donner une grande chose à la place d'une petite'(Mauss 1950: 169)[3] makes clear, I think, that Mauss by that time had come to regard the gifts given by divinity as immeasurably higher in value than those given by human beings, and in so doing was implicitly crediting gods with a precedency unattainable by mere humanity. Since a principal theme of his essay is that the act of giving elevates the status of the giver over that of the receiver and that this relationship remains unequal until – and if – the latter reciprocates with a gift of the same value,

---

This it is that provides the immortal substance on which the gods live. Thus not only is it in sacrifice that some gods are born, it is by sacrifice that all sustain their existence. So it has ended by appearing as their essence, their origin, and their creator' (Hubert and Mauss 1964 [1888]: 91).

3   '[T]hose gods who give and return gifts are there to give a considerable thing in the place of a small one' (Mauss 1990 [1950]: 17).

superiority must reside unequivocally – and perpetually – with the divine. This notion is expounded with emphatic force on page 269, where he discusses it in the particular ethnographic circumstances of the potlatch.

> *Entre chefs et vassaux, entre vassaux et tenants, par ces dons, c'est la hiér-*
> *archie qui s'établit. Donner, c'est manifester sa supériorité, être plus, plus*
> *haut,* magister; *accepter sans rendre ou sans rendre plus, c'est se subor-*
> *donner, devenir client et serviteur, devenir petit, choir plus bas* (minister).[4]

It might be remarked that most anthropological scholarship that has drawn upon the ideas advanced by Hubert and Mauss in their 'Essai sur la nature et la fonction du sacrifice' has tended to find in their paper other matters for consideration than their remarks on the hierarchical implications involved in the human–divine relationship. In one of the first monographs to apply their insights to a detailed corpus of ethnographic data, E. E. Evans-Pritchard discusses the nature of Nuer sacrifice with reference to their notion of *désacrali-sation* (1956: 198–99); their distinction between *sacrifiant* and *sacrificateur* (1956: 204); their suggestion that sacrifice establishes communication between the sacred and the profane through the vic-tim's mediation (1956: 274–75); and the contractual nature of the sacrifice, a point that Mauss was later to reinforce in the *Essai sur le don* (1950: 228–57). Twenty-nine years after the publication of *Nuer religion*, Valerio Valeri in his *Kingship and sacrifice: ritual and society in ancient Hawaii* followed Evans-Pritchard in finding use for their terms *sacrifiant* and *sacrificateur* (1985: 37), as well discussing their view of expiation (1985: 40), and the position of the victim as medi-ator in an act of communication between gods and humans (1985: 64–67). He remarks how Mauss and Hubert construe the sacrificial ritual as a triadic structure (1985: 72–73) and suggests that for them the meaning of the sacrifice lies in an analysis of the ritual as a wider

---

4 'Between chiefs and their vassals, between vassals and their tenants, through such gifts a hierarchy is established. To give is to show one's superiority, to be more, to be higher in rank, *magister*. To accept without giving in return, or without giving more back, is to become client and servant, to become small, to fall lower (*minister*).' (Mauss 1990 [1950]: 74).

whole rather than the straightforward act of giving a prestation (1985: 67). Unlike Evans-Pritchard, though, Valeri does raise the question of hierarchy, but he concurs with Mauss's later position that the god–human relationship, though one of mutual indebtedness (1985: 66–67), is a hierarchical one that grants precedence to gods, an inequality reaffirmed by their mutual exchange of unequal gifts.

Ethnographic evidence, in the form of oral narratives from Timor-Leste, indicates to the contrary, however, and my intention in this chapter is to lend empirical support for Mauss's (and Hubert's) original proposition and offer substantive corroboration for their contention that, at least occasionally, divinity needs human intervention for its very existence. In attempting to refute Mauss's revised thesis, I shall argue that with regard to their gods it is by no means invariably the case that human beings grant them a perpetual super-ordination.[5] The

---

5   It is possible that Mauss (with Hubert) intended his remarks on the traditional priestly canons (principally the texts of the *Brahmanas* and the 'Priestly Code of the Bible') to apply exclusively to these ancient texts and therefore could not be said to be generalizing about sacrifice. However, my view that Mauss was attempting to identify properties of the sacrifice as a ubiquitous ritual practice not simply offering an interpretation limited to these texts (including the Hebraic) accords with the understanding of his intention reached by others. Evans-Pritchard regarded Mauss as using the texts to postulate a 'grammar' of the sacrifice and analysed his own ethnographic data on Nuer sacrificial rituals accordingly (*Nuer Religion*, 1956: 198, 275–76) and Durkheim, in his *The Elementary Forms of the Religious Life* (1965 [1912]: 377–79), appeared to have no hesitation in drawing on their findings to interpret Spencer's and Gillen's Aranda material. More recently, in the monograph mentioned earlier, Valeri subjects Hubert and Mauss's analysis of sacrificial rituals to a very intense scrutiny (see Valeri 1985: 64–67, especially, but see also pp. 72–73) without so much as even intimating that anything in their study should be taken as applying exclusively to the particularities of Brahmanic theory. He appears, as I do, to regard their classic work as unquestionably using the priestly texts for the purpose of formulating something like a theory of the sacrifice in general rather than a more restricted exegesis of the texts themselves. Indeed, on the evident understanding that Hubert and Mauss intended their findings to have wider applicability than the particularities contained in these texts, Valeri, on p. 66, specifically discusses the issue of status between gods and human beings in a comparative context. Then we have the forthright dec-

Timorese data are especially telling because on Timor life is believed to derive ultimately from the spiritual world and so its denizens may be considered superior. Yet occasionally human beings give themselves the opportunity to reflect upon – and perhaps go so far as to actually challenge – the value they accord divine status. One way by which this may be accomplished was suggested in Chapter 4 where we saw how indigenous assumptions about the relative statuses of gods and humans might be subject to reflection seriously enough so as to put human beings in 'the driver's seat', so to speak, thereby securing for themselves an transitory precedence.[6] In this way was the hierarchical imbalance between gods, who in most circumstances are indeed accorded precedence, readjusted for a while in humanity's favour. The ritual made this reversal of status possible by human agency using the authority of ritual to restore life to a hapless local water god (*we na'in*) who was in the throes of dying. In this chapter I shall develop this argument by showing that oral narratives also offer a cultural medium for countering – even denying – beliefs dominant in a society. Oral narrative can serve as an instrument of denial and provide individuals with the means of contemplating truths[7] that might otherwise go unreflected upon.

---

laration of Dan Sperber, who clearly has no doubts on the matter: 'Hubert and Mauss were applying to sacrifice in general a synthesis of Vedic and Biblical ideas' (1985: 27).

6   To the possible objection that Hubert and Mauss's work deals with the communicative medium of sacrifice whereas the present inquiry relates to a different medium of communication, namely narrative, I would remark that one distinctive interest of the Timorese narratives lies precisely in the fact that their concern with the ascription of relative status between human beings and gods/spirits is isomorphic with the same concern displayed in certain Timorese rituals (see Hicks 1996). And for all its hyperbolic gusto I would also call attention to Leach's celebrated assertion that myth and ritual 'say' the same thing (1954: 13). Then, for that matter, does not Mauss himself use the Sanskrit and Hebraic *texts* as empirical support for his analysis of sacrificial *ritual*?

7   Including truths of the sort that Pierre Bourdieu calls *doxa*, which he contrasts with 'an orthodox or heterodox belief implying awareness and recognition of the possibility of different or antagonistic beliefs' (Bourdieu 1977: 164).

The explanatory value of religious reflexivity as an analytical tool is evident in the works of Carlo Severi, Eric Gable, Michael Houseman, and others.[8] A semantically rich term, 'religious reflexivity' includes among other things the notion that beliefs and ritual behaviour, as Højbjerg puts it, can 'turn back on themselves and 'reflect' upon their conditions of existence' (2002: 1). Reflecting upon the tenets of one's religion includes, of course, the possibility that adherents of a religion might find themselves revaluating the terms of their relationship with the divine and perhaps revise their relative standing with respect to their gods. Received ideas about precedence and subordination are decidedly grist for any believer's reflective mill, and it is within this context of religious reflexivity that Mauss's ambivalence about the comparative statuses of divinities and humans deserves reappraisal. Another point of departure for the present investigation emerges from the field of material culture with the intriguing proposition advanced by certain scholars that social anthropologists should be less inclined to continue holding to the conventional assumption that artefacts are little more than passive embodiments of cultural values, and as Marcel Vellinga (2004), for one, has done for houses constructed by the Minangkabau of western Sumatra, demonstrate that material artefacts have the potential to serve as agencies for interacting with, and even shaping, cultural values. As much can be said for the Timorese fishing hook, which embodies a principle that Marilyn Strathern (1988: 268–305) has determined to be in operation in Melanesian societies, namely transformation. In the narratives discussed below, transformation finds its material agency in this artefact, the visual appearance, tactile texture, and functional purpose of which make it admirably conducive to this role.[9]

---

8 As a touchstone for the interest aroused by this view of religion, see *Social Anthropology* (10: 1, 2002), a special issue devoted to religious reflexivity.

9 Cf. Daniel Miller, who refers to an object's capacity 'to transform into or elicit another object'. Accordingly, 'a tool is the potential creator of garden crops, a boy is a potential man, a shell necklace may attract another form of valuable' (1994: 400).

Oration in many forms, and frequently as an integral component of ritual performance, is a ubiquitous art form throughout practically all of eastern Indonesia, where, among many local populations, it commands an immensely popular forum for expressing – in figurative language and prosaic language alike – values of fundamental importance. Such is the case for those ethno-linguistic groups on Timor about which the appropriate ethnographic information has been recorded in their repertoire of narratives, where certain stock motifs occur and recur with some regularity.[10] One of these is the fishing hook, or some such sharp implement capable of embedding in flesh and occasioning a condition of morbidity in its victim. In these tales the fishing hook furnishes a semantic locus around which cluster a number of what Claude Lévi-Strauss (1979: 8) might refer to as 'invariant elements' that combine and recombine in something resembling a systematically predictable manner regardless of their ethno-linguistic provenance. This is hardly surprising since the majority of these ethno-linguistic groups share a good many sociocultural features in common.[11] They classify cosmic categories according to a dualist format; they have a penchant in narrative for devising ontological transformations of various kinds (especially from animal to human, human to animal, spirit to human, human to spirit); they have at their command a complex of beliefs regarding the creative/destructive potential of spirits; they transmit rights and duties unilineally, and operate systems of affinal alliance in which the roles of wife-givers and wife-takers are mutually exclusive. Furthermore, their beliefs include notions (effectuated ritually) concerned with life, fertility, and abundance.[12] These essentials are deemed in the last resort to be under the control of divinities and

---

10 To mention only two in addition to the motif of the hook: there is the thematic contrast between the horizontal axis and the vertical axis (Hicks 1987) and also the concept of the cycle (Hicks 1998).

11 See the monographs on the Ema (Renard-Clamagirand 1987), Mambai (Corte-Real 1998), Fataluku (Campagnolo 1979); Tetum (Hicks 1984; Sá 1961), and Bunak (Berthe 1972).

12 A detailed discussion of life, fertility, and abundance is provided in Hicks (2004).

spirits[13] whose power to confer them on – or withhold them from – human beings means that the generating source of life may be said to reside in the domain of the spirit. The geographical location of this domain varies according to the literary or ritual context in which it is evoked, but – as we have already learned – is most often said to lie underground or underwater (be it in the saltwater of the sea or the freshwater of streams, rivers, springs, or ponds), though it may also be located on an island, in the sky, or on top of a mountain. In this unseen world are believed to dwell several categories of spiritual entities, which are construed in certain narrative plots as refractions of an all-encompassing goddess (*rai inan*) who is identified with the earth and whose attributes are refracted through these spirits as distinct functions (cf. Hicks 2004: 31–3). These spiritual entities include (but are not limited to) ancestral ghosts (*mate bein*) and agricultural elementals (*klamar*).

Another category of spirit identified in the Tetum language is the *we na'in*, a designation translatable as 'lord of the water', whose telluric counterpart is the *rai na'in* or 'lord of the earth'. *We na'in* are the principal spiritual entities that appear in these narratives and they are possessed by an ambivalent moral quality. Although they may confer benefits on humans fortunate or clever enough to survive an encounter with them, a person who becomes subject to their ire may become afflicted with all manner of misfortune, most commonly sickness and infertility. Even death may befall. In manifesting themselves in the material world *we na'in* most typically adopt the guise of an aquatic creature such as an eel, a crocodile, a shark, or a turtle, but may appear as a bird. Some are the ancestors of named descent groups, and in such instances ritual sacrifice is an essential component of their relationship with their human kin. I shall return to the question of divinity-as-cultural hero shortly, when I describe the special relationship that younger brothers have with the hidden realm.

---

13 The distinction between 'gods' and 'spirits' is not always apparent in Timorese religious thinking and I use either term without implying any systematic distinction in these terms when discussing other-worldly entities.

If the fishing hook is the material artefact upon which the common plot of these narratives may be said to hinge, then the plot's nexus of sociological articulation is the relationship between the elder brother and the younger brother, perhaps juridically the most consequential in Timorese society.[14] With the exception of certain populations in the central part of the island, hereditary rights devolve through the male line for the majority of Timorese ethnic groups. Residence is patrilocal in most cases and the ideal arrangement is one in which male agnates reside as a co-resident group, but practical contingencies can militate against its realization.

One is a combination of the sociological and the psychological in that the duties male agnates owe one another can impose such a weighty burden as to impair their personal relationships and disrupt their co-residency. This threat to fraternal harmony is exacerbated by the authoritarian character implicit in the elder brother–younger brother relationship, as well as in the father–son relationship, which may bring about tensions that eventually lead to fission within the group. A classic scenario – illustrated to effect in Narrative 4 and Narrative 5 below – occurs when a younger brother breaks away from his senior to set up residence elsewhere. In this system of rights and duties the elder brother is securely wedded to the world of materiality, which is a domain in which authority is unequivocally invested in him. In this workaday world he exercises jural authority over his younger siblings and elder sisters, acting, when occasion necessitates, as a surrogate father with all the authority that Timorese societies invest in that role. In accordance with this status, the elder brother enjoys the most favourable rights in the inheritance of land, animals, and money, in addition to being first in line to succeed to a father's incumbency in political office. Within the patrilocal group, females are regarded as having a special relationship with the spiritual world and in some communities serve as ritual mediators between the two worlds. Of distinct significance in religious thought is that to some extent the same is held to be true of younger brothers, who, unlike

---

14 See Chapter 2.

their seniors, are regarded as more attuned to the spiritual realm, so that on occasions when a woman is unavailable to serve the ritual needs of a sibling group, the younger brother will serve in her stead as mediator between the human world and that of the spirits.[15]

But it is in oral art that the younger brother's spiritual connection is most conspicuously forged, and in the following narratives this association is made with dramatic verve. The younger brother's ambiguous character is exhibited in plenitude and as the plot common to all variations advances we see him, though as a human being rooted in the material world, nevertheless intervening effectively and with a measure of influence in the domain of the spirit. Many Timorese narratives revolve around the theme of an intrusion by the junior brother into the hidden world, but one in particular – a charter myth – is especially significant for the present discussion. This tale describes the foundation of the clan of the eel (Tuna) and comes from Caraubalo *suku*, Viqueque. The kinship group is said to have been founded by a cultural hero named Ali-iku, the youngest of seven brothers (Hicks 1984: 24–27), who, in imparting the descent group's sociological charter to his senior siblings, instructed them in ritual, thereby empowering them and their descendants with the capacity to communicate with the spiritual domain. The tension latent in the elder brother–younger brother relationship informs the narrative from beginning to end and culminates in the eldest brother hacking the younger brother's *alter ego*, an eel, into pieces. Ali-iku, who up to that point in the tale has exercised the conventional deference due his elder brother, then commences to transform himself into the apparently dead eel. As the transformation is taking effect, the younger-brother-eel creature gradually begins to reverse the status relationship that Ali-iku, *qua* younger brother, previously had with

---

15 A more comprehensive account of the connection between femininity and the younger brother appears in Hicks (1984: 100–102). While one might be tempted perhaps to see – in the functional complementarity of these two brothers – the local expression of a Dumèzilian-type dual sovereignty of the sort that has been described for other parts of the Indonesian archipelago, its absence of systematic institutional expression argues against this construction.

his senior siblings and starts to issue his authoritative instructions. These he supplements with further mandates, one being the proscription that henceforth none of the descendants in the male line of the newly-created Eel clan can bear the eldest brother's name. Before his brothers' astonished gaze, he completes his epiphany by transforming entirely into the eel and diving down into the depths of a sacred stream, which is his conduit to the spiritual world. His brothers then realize that he was a *we na'in* all the time.

Elsewhere (Hicks 1988) I have described narratives that take advantage of the younger brother's position as a mediator between humanity and spirits to promote the motif of the younger brother-as-hero. One popular plot portrays him as socially marginalized or being morally stigmatized by some mishap that prompts him into embarking on a picaresque adventure in the course of which he travels through or over water to penetrate the spirit realm. Enabled by an agile mind[16] and fortified by a capacity for duplicity, the quick-thinking lad responds resourcefully to the challenges that confront him during his journey and is able to exploit the opportunities that come his way. As a result, he emerges from his adventure either commanding a higher social status or finding himself a good deal more personally advantaged in various other ways than when the narrative commenced (Hicks 1988: 807). Other variants of these tales depict him as remaining in the spirit world, where he enjoys a privileged place. The narratives considered here belong to this genre, and possess the qualities of being both cosmological statements and commentaries about precedence, authority, agnatic relations, and affinal alliance.

Although the relationship between the two brothers supplies the principal sociological impetus driving the plot, their relationship is only one of several elements that impart a conjoint identity to them and invest them with their singular character. As I intimated earlier, while not all of these elements necessarily cohere into a single set in every tale, they together constitute a repertoire of standard images that lend consistent and even definitional structure to the narratives

---

16 Like Monkey in the 'Monkey Tales'.

considered as a group. In tabulated mode these elements may be summarized thus:

- The narrative begins with a residential sibling group, which may or may not include sisters.
- The younger brother's subservience to the elder brother is emphasized.
- The senior brother in the sibling group (in the third narrative it is a younger brother, but in this case he is living independently of the senior sibling) owns a fishing hook (or an equivalent artefact).
- The younger brother loses the hook (usually that of his elder brother's) while fishing.
- The younger brother seeks to retrieve it.
- The younger brother enters a sub-aquatic world, which is the world of the spirits.
- The younger brother learns that an important inhabitant of the spirit world is dying or otherwise languishing.
- The younger brother discovers that his hook (or equivalent) is responsible for the sickness.
- The younger brother cures the sickness, and by so doing gives the gift of life, or revitalization, to the god.
- The younger brother deceives the spirits into believing that the cause was some sharp natural object that he has substituted for the elder brother's hook.
- The younger brother is rewarded with an abundance of resources by the god.
- The younger brother, bolstered by his new resources, undergoes a radical improvement in social status and/or wealth.

Of the five narratives below, four come from ethno-linguistic groups speaking vernaculars that comprise part of the Austronesian family of languages and the fifth comes from a people speaking Bunak, a non-Austronesian language.[17] Regardless of language, the art of narration and the recitation of verse, especially as components

---

17 The most useful and concise study of Timor-Leste languages is Hull (1997; 2000; 2004).

of ritual or in traditional courts of law, are of pervasive importance in Timor public life, and for that matter throughout eastern Indonesia in general.[18] The Tetum language contains a number of literary categories, and the narratives discussed here are classed as *aiknananoik*, tales that among other types of story include what in English would usually be called 'myths'. As explanations of how certain natural features of the landscape and society came into existence and how various things became *lulik* some *aiknananoik* are believed to have been created by the ancestors and transmitted from generation to generation to the present. Some, like the Ali-iku tale, are the property of descent groups, for which they provide charter testaments justifying specific jural or ritual rights over which the social group is asserting claim. Except for the Ali-iku story, the narratives in the present study lack such proprietary entitlements, however, and are open to a greater measure of creativity on the part of narrators. *Aiknananoik* are most typically narrated on public occasions by *lia na'in*. For descent groups and their wife-givers and wife-takers the most important of these rituals are those carried out at birth, marriage, and death, but more encompassing community involvement occurs at calendrical ceremonies when *lia na'in* share the spotlight with priests (*dato lulik*), who are the principal ritual officiants.[19] A popular location for *lia na'in* is under the shade of a banyan tree.[20] In the jural field and political arena the significance of these figures[21] is felt in traditional *suku* where the king or *suku* chief has at his side the

---

18 Field research has shown the importance of oral literature in traditional Timorese society. Louis Berthe's (1972) study of the Bunak narratives immediately comes to mind, as does Father Sá's (1961) collection of Tetum texts, both of which I have drawn upon for the present article. For ethnic groups elsewhere in eastern Indonesia two of the most ethnographically detailed monographs, Webb Keane's (1997) on the Anakalang of Sumba and Andrea Katalin Molnar's (2000) on the Hoga Sara of Flores, attest to the importance of verbal art in the cultures of the archipelago.

19 Cf. Chapter 4.

20 Cf. Chapter 4.

21 Women are rarely 'lords of the word', but I am informed there are some in East Timor.

most respected community *lia na'in*, who as repository of customary law serves as the chief's legal councillor and makes sure that the chief 's rulings are not discordant with the words of the ancestors. Outside these formal situations 'lords of the word' function more generally as transmitters of tradition[22] and are the most authoritative voice for imparting the accumulated wisdom of a community's forebears to the local populace.

The narratives recorded below are summaries of longer tales, and in some instances, such as Narrative 5, constitute episodes in a lengthy series of episodes that are part of the complete story.[23]

THE NARRATIVES

The first narrative comes from Samoro, a Tetum-speaking population in the south-central area of East Timor (Sá 1961: 44–65).

Narrative 1

An elder brother and his younger brother enjoyed sea-fishing together. One day, however, the elder brother remained home and so his younger brother asked his brother's wife to lend him his brother's fishing hook to fish. She handed it over, but warned him not to lose the hook because if he did her husband would be angry. The younger brother went off to fish. A big fish snatched up the hook, but severed the line and escaped with the fishing

---

22 It is not to be supposed, however, that the fund of oral tradition available to a community is in any way 'owned' by these 'lords of the word' as myths may be owned by clans. Any person is at liberty to recite stories to a private audience or – if they wish to gain community recognition as 'lords of the word' themselves – in the presence of a wider public. Origins specific to individual descent groups, however, are an altogether different matter and would not normally be recited by members of other descent groups – except perhaps to, and at the behest of, the inquiring ethnographer!

23 Worth noting, I think, is that each narrative is replete with images that suggest insights into indigenous ideas other than those considered for inquiry here and that these merit consideration in their own right, like the aforementioned theme of the cyclical journey to the world of the spirits (Hicks 1988).

hook in his mouth. This fish was really the only daughter of a king who ruled over an island. Returning home the younger brother offered his brother his own hook as replacement for the hook that he had lost, but his brother was angry and refused the substitute. He ordered the junior man go and find it. To start his quest the younger brother cast a fishing-net into the sea, threw himself on it, and was borne along the surface until he came to the island over which the king ruled. There he met two young women who told him that their community was grieving because the local princess had been taken ill and none seemed able to cure her. As soon as the younger brother learned that the pain was in the princess's throat, he guessed what the cause might be but merely told them he knew of a cure and would not say what it was. Along the way, as the girls were taking him through the woods to see the princess, they passed a bamboo grove and the younger brother sliced off a sliver of bamboo that was shaped like a hook. When he saw the princess he said that her eyes should be covered and that he must be left alone with her. He was obeyed and was able to confirm his diagnosis: the hook was indeed lodged in the girl's throat. Carefully extracting the artefact, he replaced it with the bamboo sliver. He called everyone to see the bamboo hook, the sight of which astounded them, and they declared that the young man had saved the princess's life. The lad asked the king for permission to leave the island, but the latter urged him to remain a while. The king asked his subjects how best to reward the young man, and they told him that since he was growing old and there was no man to look after the kingdom, he should give their unexpected benefactor his daughter's hand in marriage and make him king. The king made this proposal to the younger brother, who agreed but asked that he be allowed to return for a time to the mainland to see his elder brother. Using the net, as before, he returned to his senior brother's house and handed over the hook. After a short stay the younger brother went back to the sea, threw out his net, and returned to the palace. There the two youngsters got married and the king delivered governance of the realm over to them.

The opening narrative establishes the main parameters by means of which the individual narratives cohere into a semantic set. The artefactual modality in which the vulnerability of divinity is revealed is shown to be the hook, and this revelation is brought about by a younger brother who, though socially disadvantaged in his own human domain, nevertheless serves notice to all who hear the story that while subordinate to his elder brother in the world of human beings, he nonetheless commands an authority in the unseen domain that is not shared by his senior, who remains safely at home in the tangible world.

Narrative 2[24]

Three brothers lived on the island of Ataúro. One day the two youngest brothers were fishing with their eldest brother's hook when it apparently became wedged in something at the bottom of the sea and was irretrievably lost. The eldest brother was angry and told them that they must find it. So the two brothers – middle and youngest – put out to sea in a canoe until they arrived near the place where they had lost the hook. The middle brother dived into the sea and saw an underwater world with his line entangled at the top of a banyan tree that was growing over a spring. He climbed the tree and spied three young women below on the ground who asked what he was doing. [The youngest of the three brothers has now vanished from the narrative. He returns as the tale ends, but in effect the middle brother now assumes the younger brother's role.] He told them he had come to find a hook that he had lost the previous night. The three women told him that the hook was stuck in the teeth of their 'grandfather' shark, who was seriously ailing. They took him to meet the sick shark. The younger brother asked the shark to open his mouth and after the fish had done so he pulled out the lost hook. The younger brother then took his leave, but before he did so he was given a reward by the shark, five betel leaves, bundled together, and tools of the blacksmith's trade.

24 The original Portuguese version of this narrative occurs in Duarte (1984: 223–24) and was collected among the Rahesuk-speaking population on Ataúro.

The shark advised the younger brother that when he reached the beach that he should turn around and let the bundle of betel leaves fall behind him and that they would be transformed into fishes. He complied and the betel was converted into a school of fish, which soon increased abundantly. He was then reunited with his brothers and together they seeded the garden that they jointly owned with only five grains of maize, five beans, and five peas. Yet from this modest seeding they had the greatest harvest they had ever known.

Using the middle brother to carry the plot is unusual in 'hook' narratives, however, and in the majority the hero of the story is a younger brother or the youngest brother of a group of siblings. He returns to this role in the next tale, which opens with him displaying the same talent for duplicity that he demonstrated in Narrative 1, though this time it is not rewarded with the same success. As the narrative unfolds, however, he regains his touch.

Narrative 3[25]

A couple had seven children. Six of them laboured daily in their gardens but the youngest son preferred to enjoy himself hunting. Every day, after hunting, he would rub soil over his body and onto his machete and pretend to his parents that he, too, had been busily at work. Suspecting deceit of some kind, however, his father spied on him one day and saw his most junior son hunting. That night the lad's mother put excrement on his plate as punishment. Furious, he went off to live by himself. In his new location the youngest brother made a garden in which he grew areca and betel. In time he married. He also began fishing in the sea. One day he impaled an unusually heavy fish on his hook. But it broke the line. He was most unhappy, but to make things worse the following day

---

25 I have previously given full English translations (from the original Portuguese) of this narrative and Narrative 4 (Hicks 1988). Narrative 3 appeared originally in Pascoal (1967: 132–37). The story's ethno-linguistic classification is Austronesian, almost certainly Tetum or Ema.

he discovered that someone was stealing areca and betel from his garden. So the next night he lay in watch for the thief. Around dawn he noticed a cockatoo fly into the garden, where it transformed itself into a man, who then helped himself without restraint to all the areca and betel he wanted. When confronted, the cockatoo-man explained that he was stealing on behalf of his queen, who was seriously wounded, and that the areca and betel were only medicines to cure her. The youngest brother did not believe him, so the cockatoo-man offered to take him to the queen's palace. They went to the beach, where the cockatoo-man told the man to close his eyes. Moments later he told him to open them. The youngest brother miraculously found himself in the palace where he confirmed what he had begun to suspect. The hook was the culprit. He announced that he could cure the queen but needed to go into the forest to think about a remedy. Upon returning, the younger brother said that he must consult alone with the patient, otherwise the remedy would fail. When the queen's attendants had gone he pulled out the hook so adroitly that not even the queen herself saw exactly what he had done, and when the attendants returned he held up a thorn he had taken from a palm-tree when he was alone in the forest. This, he claimed, was what had caused their queen's pain. As a reward the queen told the younger brother to return home and there make seven corrals. She instructed him to construct them so that the latest one built was more capacious than its predecessor, thus making the seventh the largest. The man then found himself on the beach by the same marvellous process that had originally carried him to the queen's palace. He went home to work strenuously building the corrals. When the younger brother had finished he went to the beach, where he found awaiting him the cockatoo-man, who told him to close and open his eyes. In an instant he found himself again before the queen, who said that, having built the corrals, he must now return home to make two large baskets. One he was to fill with beans; the other he was to leave empty. The youngest brother was told that sometime before dawn he was to place one basket to the right of the entrance to one of the corrals and the other basket to the left. He should leave the entrances of each corral wide open. The queen promised that countless buffaloes would soon appear and that each time a beast entered the corral the youngest brother should toss a bean from the full basket into the empty basket. When the supply of beans was exhausted, so, too, would be the number of buffaloes. The youngest brother returned home in what was by now his customary manner to carry out his orders. At dawn he heard a thunderous noise that resounded like a tempest coming off the sea and all the palm-trees around shook. The buffaloes were on the march and coming! Without anyone guiding them they began one by one entering the corrals and continued doing so for many hours until there were as many animals in the corrals as there were beans. When only a single bean remained, the last buffalo entered into the seventh corral. He was an imposing specimen, indeed the largest of all the buffaloes with horns so huge they grazed the entrance as he passed through, causing a huge rumble that made all seven corrals tremble. Once he was inside the corral the gates of all the corrals closed by themselves. The young man then gathered up the baskets, which were henceforth regarded as sacred objects. In the entire region no one was as rich as this younger brother.

In the next narrative the thief puts in a second appearance, but now in the guise of a cockatoo woman. The tale also registers the episode of the augmenting buffalo herd in the corral and continues the theme of divinity and humanity engaging in an exchange of benefits. Here, though, we find the divine lord of the water explicitly placing himself in a position of subordination to the younger brother by requesting (and receiving) from the latter the gift of a wife. A Timorese wife-taker, of course, is of inferior status to his wife-giver; indeed, their social inequality is a defining component of the relationship. That divinity should be consigned to the inferior role surely might invite listeners to the narrative to, at least, some contemplative reflection about the comparative status of gods and mortals.

Narrative 4[26]

A man of royal lineage had a daughter and two sons. One day, while his elder brother was gardening, the younger brother took the elder brother's fishing hook and went to fish at a spring locally considered *lulik*. A crocodile seized the fishing hook, which stuck in its throat and was torn from the fishing line. The elder brother demanded compensation. Now it happened that the younger brother grew betel in his garden and sometime after he lost the hook he found that some of his betel leaves had been stolen and discovered that a cockatoo woman was the thief. The cockatoo woman explained that she was collecting them to cure her grandfather, a crocodile, who had sustained a mysterious injury. The younger brother inquired about the wound and learned the injury was in the throat. When he told the cockatoo woman he might be able to cure the grandfather's wound she invited him to accompany her to attempt a cure. The younger brother cut a piece of palm-leaf that had spines attached and hid it in a fold in his sarong. When they were ready to leave, the cockatoo woman instructed him to close his eyes, which he did, and when he opened them he found himself already in her house. There the younger brother saw the ailing crocodile languishing on the ground. The man ordered everyone in the room to leave and told the crocodile to close his eyes. Immediately he had done this, the younger brother extracted the hook from its mouth, hid it in his sarong, and by the time the crocodile opened his eyes he was able to produce the piece of spiny palm-leaf and declare this object was what had caused the injury. The crocodile asked him what he wanted as a reward and the younger brother replied that he wished for a buffalo herd. The crocodile told him to build a corral. When the lad had done as he had been told the crocodile ordered him to close and open his eyes seven times. Each time he did so buffaloes appeared and kept appearing until the herd completely

26 Duarte (n. d.). This narrative likely comes from Tetum or Ema traditions and was kindly made available to me by Father Duarte, whom I thank together with the original narrator.

filled the corral. Then the crocodile himself made a request of the younger brother. He desired a woman. The young man offered him a slave, but the crocodile preferred a princess of the same blood as the young man, and so the younger brother gave the crocodile his sister as a wife.

As remarked earlier, these four narratives derive from Timorese populations speaking Austronesian languages, but the motif of the hook transcends this language family. Our next tale, from the non-Austronesian-speaking Bunak, is one such instance. In this tale both elder brother and younger brother have claims upon the impaling instrument, a golden arrow, which replaces the fishing hook as the mediating object that inducts the junior brother into the spiritual realm and imperils the life of the divinity. Nevertheless, the senior brother is its custodian and has the power to grant or deny the arrow to his inferior sibling. The sociological and psychological tensions latent in the elder brother–younger brother relationship manifest themselves more sharply than in the previous four narratives and in their lethal character recall the fate of Ali-iku-as-eel. In this version of the hook motif, the god of the underwater world appears in avian guise.

Narrative 5[27]

Two brothers who lived together caught a pair of wild pigs that were eating their garden crops but once captured the animals transformed themselves into two girls whom the elder brother married. Disgruntled that his brother refused to allow him a girl, the younger brother departed their ancestral home with his buffaloes to settle elsewhere. There he built a corral. One day a crow flew into the corral and pecked the backs of the buffaloes severely enough to inflict wounds. His onslaught so irked the younger brother that he went to his senior sibling to request the blowpipe and golden arrow they had jointly inherited as heirlooms from their father. When the crow returned to continue pecking the buffaloes

---

27 The original text of this narrative in the vernacular, together with a French translation, forms part of a very much longer Bunak text (Berthe 1972: 56–58)

the younger brother shot the golden arrow into him, but, though impaled by the arrow, the bird flew away. The younger brother searched high and low for the arrow but without ever recovering it. One day another bird told him that he knew where it was and with the younger brother astride his back the bird flew towards a lake. Reaching the lake it flew straight into the water and perched at the top of a tree below which were many people collecting water. They informed the two travellers that the local crow-king was wounded. No one could cure him. The people asked the newcomers if they knew of a cure and the visitors asked to examine the invalid. Man and bird diagnosed the wound as resulting from the golden arrow, but kept the diagnosis to themselves. Informed by this discovery the younger brother went into the woods, where he made an ar-row-head from a piece of bamboo and collected the ingredients for making betel juice. Before returning to the invalid the man chewed the betel, applied the betel juice to the wound, extracted from it his arrow-head, and hid it in his clothing. He smeared the bamboo arrow-head with his saliva to redden it with the betel juice, and then showed it to the crow-king and his retainers, telling them that here was the cause of the crow-king's incapacitation. Night after night the younger brother kept applying his medicinal betel juice to the wound until the crow-king was fully cured. During the nights when the younger brother worked at curing the crow-king the islanders would dance until dawn, among them two beautiful princesses. But during the day no one was about. The younger brother was curious as to why this was so. Now it happened that at the centre of the dance place there was a tree abounding in oranges during the day and with a pair of ripe fruits growing at the top, yet at night was virtually empty of fruit. The younger brother decided to find out where all these folk were coming from and what be-came of the oranges. So one evening he hid himself in a secluded spot from which to see the tree. After some time had passed he saw one by one the oranges begin to descend to the ground and as they did so they transformed themselves into human beings who then started to dance. When it was the turn of the two ripe oranges

116

at the top of the tree they transformed themselves into the two princesses. Eventually, after the crow-king's wound had completely cured, he wished to reward the younger brother and asked him what he desired most. The younger brother said he wished to have the two ripe oranges. The crow-king consented and augmented his gift with a piece of well-folded cloth, a fan, a thin broom, and a horn full of palm oil. He warned the younger brother to take care not to put the two oranges directly on the ground but always to make sure he placed them on the cloth. When the time came for him to leave, the younger brother again sat on the bird's back and the two companions flew off in the direction of the upper-world. Once there they stopped at a spring. Leaving the two oranges on the well-folded cloth, as instructed, the younger brother bathed while his bird-companion flew away. As he was bathing he heard peals of laughter coming from young girls but could not see them. The laughs floated across the air a second time, and the younger brother called out to whoever was there to watch out for the two oranges and not to take them or spoil them. He went on bathing but heard the laughs again. This time he spotted the two young princesses sitting on the cloth. They asked if he could not recall seeing them dance in the underworld, whereupon the younger brother recognized them and realized that the oranges must have transformed themselves into these two gorgeous creatures. The three then travelled to the elder brother's residence where the elder brother asked his younger brother to give him one of the lovely girls in exchange for one of his own wives. When the younger brother refused his brother killed him but later with the help of the fan and broom, and by applying the crow-king's palm oil to the corpse, the two princesses restored the younger brother to life. Together they then killed the elder brother, and the younger brother took his elder brother's two widows as wives.

As in Narratives 3 and 4, betel functions as a device that motivates the junior brother into a course of action relating to the spiritual world. Betel juice's recurrence in these narratives is intelligible given that on Timor this substance is the most commonly employed ritual device among all ethno-linguistic groups for establishing communication between human beings and spiritual entities.

THE HOOK, BROTHERS, AND DIVINITY

Although the elder brother–younger brother relationship is the prime sociological locus of these narratives, the plot's material crux, and perhaps even defining feature, is once more the fishing hook, the impaling instrument that by snagging, as it were, the world of divinity sets the hero on his fabulous journey. It was remarked earlier that the motif of the fishing hook (or some equivalent artefact) is found in narratives elsewhere in eastern Indonesia, where it combines sporadically with the elements identified above in addition to combining with elements that do not feature in these five narratives. Having seen how these elements come together in them, let us now take a look at how the fishing hook motif is used in three narratives outside of Timor and in three other Timorese narratives. On Flores, another Austronesian-speaking population, the Nage (Forth 1998: 39), use as the water creature an eel rather than a shark or crocodile in their stories, although in a broad sense a concordant pattern of events unfolds. Then there is a narrative from the Austronesian-speaking Atoni of West Timor (Middlekoop 1958) which relies upon the hook motif as the focus for its plot but apparently without resorting to the elder brother–younger brother relationship. Still other variants of the fishing hook motif occur on Sumba and in the Kei Islands. In the latter we find a tale in which the owner of the hook and the man who loses it live in the sky rather than on land, and no spirit-creature suffers impalement (Langen 1902, cited by van Wouden 1935: 41). As a final example, which returns us to Timor, Father Artur Basílio de Sá (1961: 88–103, 104–13) transcribes two Tetum versions of a story that tells of the mythological arrival of the first missionary on Timor, variants that have as their instrument of impalement not a hook but a ship's anchor. The anchor's function in the plot is to 'snare' the island's people and in doing so conjoin Timorese society with a spiritual agency hailing from across the sea in the person of a missionary-stranger. Duplicity enacts its role again since the stranger transforms the indigenous community that he encounters from heathendom into Christianity by means of a trick for which an anchor serves as the material agency of impalement. Repulsed by the unwelcoming populace, the priest is in the process of returning to his ship, which is preparing to weigh anchor, when a massive earthquake convulses the island. So dreadful is the trembling of the ground that the Timorese are traumatized into thinking that the ship is pulling them to the other world, and, racked by terror, they agree to convert. The visitant never enlightens them about the true nature of the phenomenon and so, as in the case of the younger brother's hook, the act of deception remains a secret.

Like the younger brother,[28] the hook is ambiguous in its intrinsic properties, its function, and its association with humanity. It is an artefact of culture manufactured from a natural resource[29] to perform a natural act, that is, catching fish, in order to sustain the lives of humans. And although it is owned – or in some manner otherwise controlled – by the elder brother, the artefact is nevertheless used and lost by the younger brother. This quality of ambiguity enables it to serve as a compelling material force for exercising human intervention in the world of the spirits. The intrusion is emphatic, and sharply invasive in a quite literal sense since its immediate function is to impale a divinity, which thereby begins to languish. By his ownership of the hook, which links him with his younger brother's adventurous passages between the material and the spiritual, the elder brother is co-opted into the plot, but as a representative of the human world. He may accordingly be understood as standing for the wider society, and in this capacity what would otherwise

---

28 And, for that matter, the missionary who is both spiritual and human.

29 One perceptive reader has drawn my attention to the fact that most artefacts are made from materials in nature. The point is well taken; however, in the stories in which a natural object, such as a sharp piece of vegetation, duplicitously replaces the fishing hook it appears to me that the replacement suggests that the story-teller is making an explicit contrast between a 'cultural' barb and a 'natural' barb.

be merely a personal relationship between younger brother and a god is made into something like a covenant between divinity and humanity. In this cosmic contract the artefact operates as a dynamic agency mediating between the two modes of existence and affecting a social transformation of profound social importance. Despite at the beginning of the narrative being cast as socially inferior, marginalized, and even despised, by the time the story ends the younger brother has emerged with a fundamentally transformed status. He now has precedence over his elder brother.

Considered as cosmological testaments, therefore, narratives that depend for their plot upon the motif of the hook provide almost as explicit an insight into indigenous thinking about religious beliefs as they do when considered as sociological commentaries since they define the hierarchical nature of the relationship between human beings and spirits. As verbal reinforcement of the ritual expression of this relationship to which attention was drawn in Chapter 5 they signify the possibility that although human beings do indeed need the gifts that divinity alone can provide and are therefore contingent upon divine favour,[30] spirits, too, must have their resources replenished, a replenishment humanity provides. As Hubert and Mauss had originally argued, then, while in the final analysis human beings may be beholden to their gods for life, fertility, and abundance, the human–divine relationship is one in which there is room for a dialogue about relative status – sufficient scope indeed to enable human beings to reflect upon those occasions when divine indisposition enables mortals to reverse the terms of their relationship and even if for only a time to claim precedence over their gods.

---

30 The water god does of course reciprocate with prestations of his own, but the respective values of the two gifts are unequal. Whereas the divine gifts merely augment the younger brother's (albeit meagre) resources and improve his (admittedly rather abject) social standing, those proffered by the man amount to a far more substantial gift as demonstrated by their power to revitalize the life of the ailing god.

CONCLUSIONS

Current arguments to the effect that material artefacts can be seen as interactive agencies that mould culture by influencing its values are confirmed by the present study. In the five narratives in this chapter, by transforming both the social identity and the cosmological character of the younger brother and thereby affecting values attributed to this social figure, the fishing hook may be regarded as constituting one such agency. Why a hook (or hook-like object) should be the artefact chosen to embody Timorese values instead of some other material object is a question open to debate, but I think that one possible answer can be found in its visual appearance and tactile nature, which lend it plausibility as an instrument for conveying the notion of snagging. These material qualities are reinforced by the practical function that the fishing hook is called upon to fulfil in the mundane world of subsistence, namely catching fish. Indeed, this instrument is manufactured for the express purpose of doing exactly that, an intention that adds further suitability to its function as a tool for conveying metaphorically the notion of snagging divinity and thereby functioning as an agent of transformation. In these narratives, accordingly, the fishing hook may be understood as the artefactual expression of a local mode of culturally constructing, what Daniel Miller (1994: 400) has described as the 'order of things', that is to say, a modality in which an artefact becomes the material instrument for bringing about transformations of ontological and sociological significance. Although it would be too much of a stretch to claim that narrative has gone unremarked in the context of religious reflexivity, as Severi (2002: 23) makes plain in his observations on the work of Kristof Pomian, Jack Goody, and Vladimir Propp, discussions about the concept's explanatory capacity emphasize its capacity to shed light in fields of social and individual experience other than narrative. For example, in the 2002 special issue of *Social Anthropology* (see note 8), we find such topics as healing (Lewis 2002), ritual language (Severi 2002), play and scepticism (Gable 2002), sacrifice (Højbjerg 2002), initiation rites (Houseman 2002), and transmission frequency (Whitehouse 2002) dealt with rather than narratives of the genre considered here. The authors make plausible cases for the applicability of the concept for their respective fields of interest, certainly, but narrative, more especially in the form of myth, has failed to earn the due to which I think it is entitled. I hope that the present inquiry has shown that we need to reaffirm the importance of narrative as a medium for conveying alternative views of religious tenets in addition to being a form of art that enables reflexivity to address serious concerns of the human condition. Given the willingness to reflect upon the truths of religious beliefs, societies have at their disposal the verbal resources of narrational discourse that, at the same time as providing entertainment and instruction, afford a public forum for self-conscious reflections about experience.[31]

REFERENCES

Berthe, Louis 1972. *Bei Gua: itinéraire des ancêtres, mythes des bunaq de Timor*. Paris: Éditions du Centre National de la Recherche Scientifique.

Bourdieu, P. 1977. *Outline of a Theory of Practice* (transl. by R. Nice). (Cambridge Studies in Social and Cultural Anthropology 16). Cambridge: University Press.

Campagnolo, Henri 1979. *Fataluku I: relations et choix, introduction méthodologique à la description d'une langue 'nonaustronésienne' de Timor Oriental*. (Langues et Civilisations de L'Asie du Sud-Est et du Monde Insulindien 5). Paris: Centre de Documentation et de Recherches sur L'Asie du Sud-Est et le Monde Insulindien (CeDRASEMI)/Centre Nacionale de la Recherche Scientifique.

Corte-Real, B. De Araújo E. 1998. 'Mambae and its verbal art genres: a cultural reflection of Suru-Ainaro, East Timor.' Thesis submit-

---

31 The reader might here recall Victor Turner's suggestion that monster masks in central African rituals encourage contemplative reappraisals of values important in local religious thought: 'Monsters startle neophytes into thinking about objects, persons, relationships, and features of their environment they have hitherto taken for granted.' (Turner 1967: 105).

ted for the degree of Doctor of Philosophy, School of English, Linguistics, and Media, Macquarie University, Sydney.

Duarte, Jorge 1984. 'Timor: Ritos e mitos ataúros.' Lisbon: Instituto de Cultura e Língua Portuguesa, Ministério da Educação.

Durkheim. Émile 1965 [1912]. *The Elementary Forms of the Religious Life* (transl. by J. Ward). New York: Free Press.

Evans-Pritchard, E. E. 1956. *Nuer Religion*. Oxford: Clarendon Press.

Forth, Gregory 1998. *Beneath the Volcano: Religion, Cosmology and Spirit Classification among the Nage of Eastern Indonesia.* (*Verhandelingen van het Koninklijk Instituut voor Taal-, Land- en Volkenkunde 177*). The Hague: Martinus Nijhoff.

Gable, E. 2002. 'Beyond belief? Play, Scepticism, and Religion in a West African village'. *Social Anthropology* 10: 41–56.

Hicks, David. 1984. *A Maternal Religion: The Role of women in Tetum myth and ritual*. DeKalb: Northern Illinois University Center for Southeast Asian Studies.

—— 1987. 'Space, mobility, time, and symbol' in *Indonesian Religions in Transition*, ed. by Rita S. Kipp and Susan Rodgers, pp. 35–47. Tuscon: University of Arizona Press.

—— 1988. 'Literary masks and metaphysical truths'. *American Anthropologist* 90: 807–17.

—— 1996. 'Making the king divine: a case study in ritual regicide from Timor'. *Journal of The Royal Anthropological Institute* (new series.) 2: 611–24.

—— 2004. *Tetum Ghosts and Kin: Fertility and gender in East Timor*. Prospect Heights, Ill.: Waveland Press, Inc.

Højbjerg, C. K. 2002.'Religious Reflexivity: Essays on attitudes to religious Ideas and practice'. *Social Anthropology* 10: 1–10.

Houseman, M. 2002. 'Dissimulation and simulation as forms of religious reflexivity'. *Social Anthropology* 10: 77–89.

Hubert, H. and M. Mauss 1888. *Essai sur la nature et la fonction du sacrifice. L'Année Sociologique* 2: 29–238.

—— 1964 [1888]. *Sacrifice: its nature and function* (transl. by W. D. Halls). Chicago: University of Chicago Press; London: Cohen and West Ltd.

Hull, Geoffrey 1997. 'Basic lexical affinities of Timor's Austronesian languages'. *Studies in Languages and Cultures of East Timor* 1: 97–202.

—— 2000. 'Historical phonology of Tetum'. *Studies in Languages and Cultures of East Timor* 3: 158–212.

—— 2004. 'The Papuan languages of Timor'. *Studies in Languages and Cultures of East Timor* 6: 23–99.

Keane, Webb 1997. *Signs of Recognition: powers and hazards of representation in an Indonesian society.* Berkeley: University of California Press.

Langen, H. G. 1902. *Die Key- oder Kii-Inseln des O. I.* Vienna.

Leach, E. R. 1954. *Political Systems of Highland Burma: a study of Kachin social structure.* London: London School of Economics and Political Science, G. Bell and Sons Ltd.

Lévi-Strauss, Claude 1979. *Myth and Meaning: Cracking the code of culture.* New York: Schocken Books.

Lewis, G. 2002. 'Between public assertion and public doubts: a Sepik ritual of healing and reflexivity'. *Social Anthropology* 10: 11–21.

Mauss, Marcel 1950. '*Essai sur le don: forme et raison de l'échange dans les sociétés archaïques*'. In *Sociologie et anthropologie* (ed. by) Marcel Mauss, pp. 143–279. Paris: Presses Universitaires de France.

—— 1990 [1950]. *The Gift: The form and reason for exchange in archaic societies* (trans. W.D. Halls). London: Routledge.

Middlekoop, P. 1958. 'Four tales with mythical features, characteristic of the Timorese people'. *Bijdragen Tot de Taal-, Land- en Volkenkunde* 114: 384–405.

Miller, D. 1994. 'Artefacts and the meaning of things', in *Companion Encyclopedia of Anthropology,* Tim Ingold (ed.), pp. 396–419. London: Routledge.

Molnar, A. K. 2000. *Grandchildren of the Ga'e Ancestors: Social oganization and cosmology among the Hoga Sara of Flores.* Leiden: Koninklijk Instituut voor Taal- en Volkenkunde Press.

Pascoal, E. E. 1967. *A alma de Timor vista na sua fantasia: lendas, fábulas e contos*. Braga: Barbosa and Xavier, Lda.

Renard-Clamagirand, Brigitte 1987. *Marobo: une société Ema de Timor*. Paris: Centre National de la Recherche Scientifique.

Sá, A. Basílio de 1961. *Textos em teto literatura oral timorense*. Lisbon: Junta de Investigaçoês.

Severi, C. 2002. 'Memory, reflexivity and belief: reflections on the ritual use of language'. *Social Anthropology* 10: 23–40.

Sigaud, Lygia 2002. 'The vicissitudes of the gift'. *Social Anthropology* 10: 335–58.

Sperber, Dan 1985. *On Anthropological Knowledge: Three essays*. (*Cambridge Studies in Social Anthropology* 54). Cambridge: University Press; Paris: Éditions de la Maison des Sciences de L'Homme.

Strathern, M. 1988. *The gender of the gift*. Berkeley: University of California Press.

Turner, V. 1967. *The forest of symbols*. Ithaca, N.Y.: Cornell University Press.

Valeri, V. 1985. *Kingship and sacrifice: ritual and society in ancient Hawaii* (transl. by P. Wissing). Chicago: University of Chicago Press.

Van Wouden, F. A. E. 1935. *Sociale structuurtypen in de Groote Oost*. Leiden: J. Ginsberg.

Vellinga, Marcel 2004. 'Constituting unity and difference: vernacular architecture in a Minangkabau village'. (*Verhandelingen van het Koninklijk Instituut vor Taal-, Land- en Volkenkunde 220*). Leiden: KITLV Press.

Whitehouse, Harvey 2002.'Religious reflexivity and transmissive frequency'. *Social Anthropology* 10: 91–103.

CHAPTER 7

Impaling Spirit

Three Categories Of Ontological Domain In Eastern Indonesia

It is in the penumbra, between the clear visibility of things and their total extinction in darkness when the concreteness of appearances becomes merged in half-realized, half-baffled vision, that spirit seems to disengage itself from matter to envelop it with a mystery of soul suggestion. (Caffin 1910)[1]

It will be recalled that Tylor proposed as a minimum definition of religion 'the belief in Spiritual Beings' (1883: 424) and that '[...] under the name of Animism [he sought] to investigate the deep-lying doctrine [as he called it] of Spiritual Beings, which embodies the very essence of Spiritualistic as opposed to Materialistic philosophy' (1883: 425).[2] In the region that concerns us here the contrast between the 'Spiritualistic' and the 'Materialistic' offers us lessons in how certain societies seek to come to terms with the fact that the two ontological domains, or statuses, by their very natures,

---

1   Art and photographic critic Charles Caffin's comment on Edward Steichen's celebrated photograph, 'The Pond-Moonlight' that shows a pond in a wooded area with moonlight glinting between the trees and casting reflections on the water.

2   I wish to thank the following for their help in assisting me in this study: Dr. Lisa Palmer, Dr. Michael Prager, Dr Susanne Rodemeier, Miss Francesca Calarco, Dr Sachiko Murata, Dr Michael Ashkenazi, a reviewer of a previous version, and Professor Kaj Århem and Professor Guido Sprenger who invited a contribution from me for their panel, 'Animism in Southeast Asia', at The European Association for South East Asian Studies EUROSEAS, held in Gothenburg, Sweden, August 26–27, 2010. Thanks, too, to Ms Katharina Stöhr for her translation of Narrative 5. A special word of gratitude to José Maria Mok, who, through the considerate offices of Dr Lisa Palmer, generously permitted me to include a synopsis of the unpublished Naueti text that he collected and which makes its appearance here as Narrative 4.

are inaccessible to each other. Intrinsic to their endeavour is the notion of conjunction, i.e., the process by which the two ontological statuses are subsumed in a relationship of proximity or even syncretism, since some sort of relationship is implied by the very existence of this duality. Furthermore, although this conjunction may have a destructive aspect, it has its beneficial aspect as well, and studies in comparative religion show that more often than not the conjunctive interaction of human beings and their spirits is mutually beneficial, and from the human perspective, especially the paramount benefits accruing from involvement in the world of the spirit are life and plenitude. Securing these benefits comes about in ritual, of course. As Arthur Maurice Hocart (1954: 19) has put it:

> Rituals have as their purpose to produce or increase the necessaries of life. They are acts of creation. They create more witchetty grubs, more buffaloes, more clouds, or whatever the desired objects may be. The cosmic rites create more of everything that man may need, and as the food supply depends upon the proper working of the whole world, such ceremonies create the world.

Narrative, too, fulfils this function, and one purpose of this chapter is to demonstrate how. This much said, the question arises: how can what is insubstantial interact with what is substantial?; how can spirits, which are invisible and intangible be brought or – as I shall attempt to demonstrate in this chapter – more properly, 'thought' into a relationship with human beings, who are visible and tangible? Certain narratives in the textual repertoires of peoples of eastern Indonesia juxtapose specific motifs that recur with sufficient regularity to define them as a set. I would like to draw attention to seven such motifs: (a) water; (b) life and plenitude/abundance; (c) an instrument of impalement or entrapment, an arrow, sword, rope, fishing line, or – most typically – a fishing hook[3]; (d) the quest, usually circular; (e) the social relationship of elder brother/younger brother; (f) de-

---

3   To avoid cumbersome locution, from this point onwards, unless otherwise remarked, I shall use the term 'fishing hook' or 'hook' to include all these surrogates.

ception (successful or unsuccessful) or an error; and (g) visibility/
invisibility, as indexed by the opening and/or shutting of the eyes[4].
In the final section of his first volume of *Primitive Culture* Edward
Tylor re-emphasizes his evocation of the duality that he remarked
earlier by referring to it as 'the deepest of all religious schisms, that
which divides Animism from Materialism' (1883: 502), and it is clear
from his words that he identified the distinction between spirit and
matter as central to discussions about religion. Given his awareness,
therefore, it is interesting that Tylor paid little consideration to the
possible interfaces where the two ontological domains interplay with
each other; nor did he discuss, in a more comprehensive manner, how
the realm of the visible and the realm of the invisible are brought into
relationship in different systems of belief. In eastern Indonesia one
such interface for this kind of interplay and visible/invisible dialectic
is water, whether fresh or salt[5] and an analysis of the seven narratives summarized here makes it possible to see how the indigenous
imagination deploys a material artefact, the aforementioned fishing
hook, to convey its comprehension of the interdependence of the two
ontological domains.

Current explorations of animistic thinking among populations
living in other parts of the world highlight predation as a pervasive
motif in their thought. Among Amerindians in Amazonia (Århem
1996) the relationship between predator and prey functions as a
central motif that gives coherence to affinal bonds, ritual, and cosmology, as well as their attitudes towards the natural environment
on which they depend. For the Wari' in western Amazonia, 'Humans
provide the Water Spirit Society with new members who marry and

---

4   Each of these seven motifs appears sporadically in other narratives of the
    archipelago, either in conjunction with certain other motifs considered
    in this chapter or alone. However, in the class of narrative discussed here
    they conjoin into an identifiably cohesive set of tales, bound together by
    the repetitions of plot device, and play their respective parts in imparting
    meaning to the entire set.

5   Dr. Michael Prager (personal communication) notes that water as interface
    between spirit and matter is also a recurrent theme throughout Southeast
    Asia and the Pacific, as it is in the pre-Islamic cosmology of Bima.

bear children, enhancing the reproduction of Water Spirit Society. The Water Spirits provide the living Wari' with life-sustaining animal food. For Wari', this exchange does not only reproduce the primary human–nonhuman relations of their cosmology but also promises an enhancement of ecological resources important to their subsistence. White-lipped peccaries and fish are the only foods encountered in dense concentrations in this environment …' (Conklin 1995: 90).

These seven narratives may be seen to constitute a coherent 'set' in the sense established by Claude Lévi-Strauss (1979), in which the same few motifs are worked and reworked, at once diverse and constant, in the advancement of certain ideas important to the tellers and hearers alike. Given the desiccated nature of that region of Southeast Asia, it is understandable that water, whether fresh or salt, should come to occupy a prominent place in many narratives of eastern Indonesia. Nor, given the widespread belief in all manner of animistic forms is it at all surprising that spirits also figure recurrently. In the set of narratives identified in this analysis water is cast as the essential mediating agency for engaging the two ontological modes of spirit and matter in a reciprocal relationship in which benefits accrue to at least one or – more commonly – both parties. These benefits include life, health, fertility, elevation in social status, and plentitude. So vital is this motif that it may be regarded as the 'fulcrum' of the tales and of the entire set while the other six motifs, combining and recombining, serve as lenders of support to this central motif. As a natural substance its cultural counterpart is the hook, which operates as a 'connector', so to speak, functioning to conjoin the two metaphysical domains. In these works of imagination this connector is an instrument of impalement or capture which makes its appearance in diverse forms, most typically that of a fishing hook[6],

---

6   See Chapter 6 where I discuss the symbolic semantics of the fishing hook in the comparative context of eastern Indonesia. This analysis is intended as a second step in the investigation of this motif and its congeners. It might be noted that the motif of the elder brother and the lost fishing hook is not restricted to the Indonesian archipelago. The oldest surviving Japanese book, the *Kojiki* that dates to 712 A.D., contains a story that fits into the

the owner of which is, more often than not, a superior elder brother whose inferior younger brother, after losing the artefact, engages in a quest to retrieve it, the outcome of his venture typically inverting the terms of their relative statuses.[7]

The narratives analysed here are truncated synopses of their originals and derive from the corpus of stories that form part of the verbal traditions of Sumbawa, Flores, Kei, the Alor Peninsula, and Timor.

A few summary remarks concerning the ethnographic contexts in which the narratives discussed in this article are recited are in order. The island inhabited by the people of eastern Bima defines the western geographic boundary of the societies mentioned; the populations of the Kei islands define the eastern boundary. In between are Flores, where the Nage live, Timor, to the east, where the Meto, Makassai, and Naueti live; and just north of Timor a small island cluster dominated by Alor. The people who incorporate the fishing hook into their narratives are not necessarily fisher folk, indeed, the majority of the ethno-linguistic groups, whose narratives are discussed here, generally live at some distance from the sea, e.g., the Naueti and most Makassai and Meto populations, though locally, there may be rivers, streams, springs, or lagoons from which they may take fish and crustaceans. The subsistence of these societies is based for the most part on the swidden or irrigated cultivation of rice, maize, sweet potatoes,

---

corpus of narratives analysed here were it not for the fact that it comes from outside the ethnographic region that we are considering (see Anon. 1983). I am indebted to Miss Francesca Calarco for bringing this source to my attention. In another reference to Japan, Dr Michael Ashkenazi sent me in response to my earlier article on the younger brother and the fishing hook (Hicks 2007). He remarked: 'The 'younger brother loses the fishing hook' myth is not confined to the Indonesian archipelago. I came across it as one of the founding myths of the Japanese imperial house. In the Japanese case, at least, it forms a complex with a Japanese version of the Melusine myth, which spans Asia from east to west.'

7   It may be recalled that Christopher Booker has identified 'The Quest' as one of the seven 'basic plots' which he considers universal themes common to the human imagination. Of special interest for the present study is his discussing all seven basic plots under the rubric 'The Seven Gateways to the Underworld'.

yams, and fruits of different kinds, among other cultivars; and raising chickens, pigs, buffaloes, and cattle. Local environmental cultural differences make for variation, of course; but the alternation of wet and dry season has an immense influence on all of them. Roughly speaking, the wet season in most regions runs from about October to April while the dry season occupies the period May to September. Again, however, local variations occur and the rainfall regime is never to be counted on. Patrilineal descent and patrilocal residence tend to be the preferential modes governing social order – although the Bimanese are cognatic – accompanied by the giving of bridewealth. Regimes of matrilineal descent / matrilocal residence (accompanied by no bridewealth) occur, and there is invariably scope for a variety of permutations in between. With the exception of the Bimanese, the populations from whom these narratives come practise asymmetric alliance, whether of a prescriptive or non-prescriptive character. Prominent, of course, among the Timorese people is also the precedence of the elder brother to whom the younger brother is expected to display deference. This relationship, as we shall see, is the hinge on which almost all the plots depend. The spirit world is, for virtually all these groups, a domain populated by an array of diverse elementals which include sky gods, earth goddesses, nature spirits, agricultural spirits, and – most influential of all in daily life – ghosts of the ancestors. The appellation 'god' or 'divinity' in the case of these societies may denote a high god or a lesser manifestation of divinity, such as an animistic power residing at the bottom of the sea or some such aquatic habitat, or a local immaterial power resident at the top of a mountain or in a grove of trees. Rituals, whether of a communal nature, such as the rites of passage of birth, marriage and death, or rituals carried out at the more restricted level of the household, control much of the religious life, which in some communities is centered around local versions of the Timorese *uma luliks* that provide a physical space for communication with the ancestors. The oral and, among the Bimanese, written, literature is rich and contains a variety of genres that include myths, legends, folktales, fables, poems, songs, and ritual speech in which spirits and human beings interact.

132

THE NARRATIVES

Narrative 1

The following narrative comes from the Nage people who live in the central part of Flores. It is one of many texts that comprise their extensive oral literature and was collected by Gregory Forth (1998 38–42)[8].

> Lalo Sue, a younger brother, asked his elder brother, Siku Sue, if he might borrow his fishing hook and line. Although Siku refused, Lalo borrowed them anyway. While he was fishing at night in a pool along came a large eel that broke the fishing line, taking the fishing hook with it. Siku was furious and ordered Lalo to retrieve it. Lalo then went to his garden, which was located near the pool in which he had lost the hook and the line. Remaining there for some days he noticed that the flowers on his pumpkins were being plucked, and to find the culprit he hid himself very early one morning at the top of a tree. Just as dawn was breaking he glimpsed two fish emerge from the water in the pool. They wriggled up the bank and after shedding their skins proved to be two women. Actually, they were spirits that lived in a village beneath the waters of the pool and as they were plucking the flowers Lalo demanded to know what they were doing. They said that they were collecting a flower called *runu* (*Wedelia* species) to make a medicine to cure their father who had an injured jaw. Their father had been hit by a 'god's tooth'. Lalo instantly realized that the father must be the eel and advised them that the flowers would not cure him. But he knew a medicine that would. They said that if he did so, they would reward him. Lalo entered the water and the two women told him to hold onto their backs and keep his eyes closed. When he arrived at the gate of the underwater village Lalo opened his eyes. Arriving at the father's house Lalo saw his fishing line wrapped around a house post. He tugged the line and heard a cry of pain and as he unraveled the line saw the old man rocking back and forth. Lalo had

---

8   As with most narratives summarized here, Forth's original text is longer and contains motifs additional to the ones I specify.

brought some dried coconut with which, after he had chewed it, he used to massage the invalid's jaw. When the jaw was sufficiently soft Lalo extracted the fishing hook and the man asked Lalo how he might reward him. After some time, Lalo told him that all he wished were vine seeds that he had seen children playing with in the village plaza and an old piece of rope tied around the village gate with which to tie up the basket in which the seeds would be placed. Puzzled though he was that Lalo wanted such worthless things the old man agreed. Lalo also asked for a set of four daggers called *kamu ke'o* and these were also granted. The two fish women took Lalo back to the dry land. When he arrived at the edge of the pool near his garden Lalo peered into the basket and instead of the vine seeds he saw great round pieces of gold. Back in his village Lalo was reunited with Siku who was full of remorse for having made his younger brother look for his lost hook and line. He had thought him dead and was about to hold a wake. Lalo returned the hook and line and showed his elder brother the gold.

Narrative 2

This narrative – of which there are a number of versions – was collected by Michael Prager (2010) from Bima regency in eastern Sumbawa. The motif of the quest is not elaborated in the form of a journey explicitly undertaken but a journey between dry land and sea would seem clearly implied. The deception/error motif appears. The younger brother lies to, and then tricks, his elder brother; and the elder brother fails to pick up all the scattered sesame seeds.

In Bima lived two royal brothers. The elder brother was called Indera Kemala. The younger was called Indera Zamrut. Kemala resided in the west; Zamrut resided in the east. Because he loved to fish, Kemala's palace was located near the sea. He owned a golden fishing hook. Because he loved agriculture Zamrut's palace was located near the fields and mountains. He owned a golden tray that contained seeds. One day Zamrut visited his elder brother and asked if he could borrow his fishing hook. Kemala assented but told his younger brother to take care of the fishing hook and not lose it. However, while Zamrut was fishing in the sea the prince of the perch species (*ikan kerapu*) swallowed the fishing hook and broke the line. When Zamrut told Kemala what had occurred he was ordered to go and find it. Zamrut travelled to the sea where he found the fish in a state of great agitation. They were looking for a healer and a medicine with which to cure the perch prince whose throat was injured. He had swallowed a hook. Zamrut extracted the hook whereupon the perch prince told him he would grant any wish the younger brother might have. Zamrut told him that he was content to have cured the perch prince and asked permission to leave. He arrived ashore accompanied by a swarm of fish. Zamrut gave his brother the hook and returned home. There, he filled his golden tray with white sesame seeds which he placed above the ground at the entrance to his palace. On the ground he sprinkled some white sand and sent word to his elder brother that he was seriously ill. Kemala did come, but as he entered his younger brother's palace the golden tray fell to the floor and the white sesame seed spilt out and mixed into the white sand. Zamrut ordered his elder brother to restore the tray to its original state by separating the sesame seed from the sand. Kemala tried and looked like he had succeeded in filling the tray with the every one of sesame seeds. But in fact he had failed to do so because when Zamrut came and poured water over the sand three sprouts of sesame emerged from the ground. Realizing he had failed in his task of restoring the sesame seeds as they had originally been in the golden tray, Kemala, after wandering about aimlessly, decided to go into exile. He finally disappeared in a pond leaving his younger brother king of Bima.

A much shorter variant of this narrative is given by Michael Hitchcock (1996: 47). The perch is replaced by a whale; the fish in a state of agitation are now shrimps; they tell him that their king, the whale, is sick; and Zamrut (here called 'Jambrut') realizes that it is his elder brother's hook that is the culprit. A *pari* fish agrees to take him to the king on condition that Zamrut's descendants will never eat *pari*[9]; and when he reaches the afflicted king whale's court 'craft-ily' persuades the courtiers of the king that his cure will only work if they close their eyes. He removes the hook, conceals it, and holds up a piece of seaweed as the agency responsible for the impalement. Zamrut is observed, however, by another fish, a *tampoli*, which unlike the other spectators had kept its eyes open. For this reason it is now considered by the Bimanese to be especially difficult to catch.

Narrative 3

A water/mountain deity becomes visible in the form of a wild boar and lures a man into hunting him so as to make him thirsty, a deprivation of water that obliges the hunter to make an uneasy pact with the deity. The tale lacks the motifs of the hook and the fraternal relationship and the quest is undertaken by a woman, not a younger brother and she seeks not a fishing hook, but water with which to provide her com-munity with life and plentitude. Furthermore, her quest into the spirit realm, via water, is not of a cyclical character because ultimately she does not return. Nevertheless, her quest is undertaken through the initiative of a man, her father, who would appear to take on the role of elder brother that we see in the other narratives. The means to life for human beings and spirits alike is this woman for it is her bridewealth that makes possible the life and abundance that her community and the deity subsequently enjoy. Another feature of the tale is that the deity is wife-taker to humanity. The text was collected on the island of Pura, in the Alor Peninsula, by Susanne Rodemeier (2009).[10]

> While out hunting a huge wild boar (which was in reality the mountain/water deity metamorphosed), Olangki, father of a girl named Bui Hangi, grew very thirsty. And so, as he was passing the mountain home of the local deity, he asked it for water. He did so by thrusting his arrow into the earth saying: 'If I get enough

---

9   A taboo observed by the Bimanese royal family (Hitchcock 1994: 47).

10 Dr Rodemeier has noted that unlike in other stories the hunter does not succeed in impaling an animal nor does he lose his arrow, though he does ram it into the ground (Rodemeier 2013).

[water] for the fields also, I promise to give my daughter in exchange.'[11]. At that moment water began emerging from the earth,
clouds formed, and heavy rain began falling. Olangki realized that
he should not have said what he did and hurried home, only to
learn the rainfall had caused a huge landslide that threatened his
village. To avert this disaster Olangki told his wife to take Bui, their
daughter, up the mountain next day. Giving her to the god was the
only way to prevent calamity. The following day, as the two women
were ascending the mountain, the rain ceased. As they approached
a mountain pool Bui told her mother that she could see smoke
on the slopes. This was due to the slash-and-burning carried out
by the mountain spirits preparing their fields. Bui pointed towards
the smoke and the woman looked, but because she was human
and the smoke was of spirit essence she could not see it. When she
glanced back to where Bui had been, she found that her daughter
had disappeared into the pool. Before starting to walk down the
slippery path home Bui's mother looked for a stick with which to
support her and saw, floating on the surface of the pool, a number of
bamboo sticks. She picked up one and upon reaching home thrust
it beneath the floor of her house and fell asleep. Next morning
Olangki looked at what had been a bamboo stick and saw instead
a sacred sword. He immediately realized that the bamboo stick
was part of the bridewealth given by the deity. Bui's mother had
left most of the bridewealth; but at least she had taken something.
Now, as owner of a sacred sword, he could summon up fresh water
from the earth with a stab of his sword. Water would flow – or
cease – as he willed. The following year, before the harvest ritual,
Olangki asked his wife to invite Bui. She arrived, accompanied by
her recently-born infant which, since it was carried in a cloth, was

---

11 Parallels may be found in Lombok (Bosch 1961:155–156) and among the
Atoni (van Wouden 1968: 50). The Lombok story involves a guru who
displays extraordinary powers when he thrusts his trident into the earth
and makes a spring gush forth. For its part, the Atoni story describes how
the eldest of a group of brothers thrusts his sword into the ground and a
spring issues from it.

invisible to human eyes. Bui hung the cloth containing the baby in her mother's house and ordered her mother not to look into the cloth even were she to hear a cry issue from it. Her mother fell asleep but was woken by a strange noise that sounded somewhat like a fish. The mother was confused and looking inside the cloth saw a big red fish with a pair of appetizing eyes. Without thinking she removed an eye and ate it. Bui felt a pain in her breast and ran back to her mother's house. She saw what had happened and became very angry. She decided she could no longer stay with her parents. Nor could she ever enter the human domain again. The relationship was over forever. Bui walked uphill to a cave. This she entered and then used a boulder to seal it up. Later, Bui appeared to her father in a dream. She explained what had occurred but promised that no one from her human family would ever suffer thirst or experience hunger.

Susanne Rodemeier (2009: 472, 476) emphasizes the extreme environmental pressure that the people of Pura faced in the period in which the events described here are supposed to have occurred. They had no source of permanent fresh water, which was assured only for the three to four months the rainy season lasted. Moreover, not only had villagers to endure the 'life-threatening lack of water'; they were also subject to 'its equally dangerous abundance'. Rodemeier characterizes the god as a composite mountain and water deity. When rain begins to fall, it seems to villagers that the mountain and the clouds surrounding it are merged and that the water itself arises out of the earth – rather than fall from the sky – before cascading down the slopes. In pre-Christian times villagers credited the mountain deity with regulating the flow of water and creating the rainfall. The author remarks that on Pura the inferior status of wife-taker, a consistent feature of asymmetric alliance systems in eastern Indonesia, is magnified if it has not been completely discharged. Hence, even though it was Bui's mother who failed to collect the entire 'bridewealth' from the deity, the deity becomes so delinquent in his duty as wife-taker that he is obligated for evermore to provide water for his wife-giver's family and protect them from its excess. Another point of interest is the fashion in which Bui transforms into spirit, for she metamorphoses from a material entity into an animistic entity only gradually (Ibid. 478). Her ability to see the spirit smoke is the first indication that her transformation is beginning to take place and her ontological status now becomes ambiguous because human beings cannot normally see spirits. Bui's metaphysical ambiguity continues for some time, even after she has disappeared into the pool. 'She was still able to meet her father in his dreams and give him advice [and] could even physically meet her family', i.e., on the occasion of a ritual (Ibid.). During this ritual, while human beings could not actually see Bui's spiritual in-laws, they could glimpse 'shadows that remained in the shade of tree'. But as for Bui's baby, since it was hidden in the cloth, there was no proof that it really existed until, by infringing Bui's taboo, her mother saw with her own eyes final proof that her daughter was indeed married and because her grandchild was a red fish instead of a normal human infant she realized that its father was not of the material world. Because of her mother's error in catching sight of the hidden baby, a *faux pas* made more heinous by her eating her grandchild's eye: 'Bui had to carry out the final step in her metamorphosis into a fuller member of the supernatural world' (Ibid.). She effaces herself to the human eye and will never again return to the material domain.

Bui's transformation from human being into spirit was, it will be obvious, a process rather than an event, and a somewhat lengthy process at that. Indeed, it is the verbal equivalent of a rites of passage. Bui's initially vanishing into the pool was her stage of separation; her disappearance for good into the cave, her stage of incorporation; and the period when she moved between the two worlds, the transitional period or 'betwixt and between' stage, that of liminality.[12]

---

12 Bui's transformation into a spirit can be understood as a variation of the myth of Ali-iku, the youngest brother, who transforms himself into a spirit eel, of which I provide a complete transcription in Chapter 8. Ali-iku is male and Bui Hangi is female but both plots describe a transformation from matter into spirit; a metamorphosis that occurs gradually rather than instantly; and one that remains permanent. The nature of these transformations supports the association that I have elsewhere argued to occur between the younger brother and the female gender (see Hicks 1984: 100–102). Bui's

Narrative 4

The tale that follows was collected by Mr José Maria Mok (Palmer 2010) and comes from the Naueti, an ethnic group living in the Uato Carabau district of Timor. This narrative, too, displays the motifs of the fishing hook and the motif of the protagonist's deception: but the fishing line substitutes for the fishing hook in the mouth of the afflicted aquatic animal, which here is a 'sacred eel', while the hook itself is impaled in its gills. The protagonist is not described as a younger brother and the king would appear not to be the only eel afflicted by the fishing hook. The error motif, represented in this instance by a failure to take complete advantage of the deity's/spirit's gift, appears, and like Bui Hangi's mother, the protagonist fails to take all the proffered gifts. A further point of interest is that the gift, when it has been transformed, turns into a herd of buffaloes (cf. Narrative 7), a species of animal typically included in bridewealth.

The narrative tells of a fisherman whose palm wine kept being stolen. The culprit used to come out of a spring each night and help himself to the wine. The owner of the palm trees set a trap and caught the man responsible. He turned out to be the assistant of a king, who was a 'sacred eel' (*tuna*). The thief said he only wanted the wine to take back to his king who was sick. The king could neither eat nor drink; but after drinking the wine he was able to sleep. The owner of the palms did not believe him but the thief convinced him to follow him to the edge of the spring. He persuaded the man to shut his eyes and together they both entered the water. When the man opened his eyes he found himself in an underwater kingdom where he saw girls with scaly skins working hard. The owner of the wine was taken to the sick king and saw that he had swallowed the fishing hook and it was caught in his

---

father, it should be noted, acts with the same inept authoritarian manner as Ali-iku's elder brother and the tale thereby expresses the association that Timorese social organization makes between the father and the eldest brother, to which I draw attention in Chapter 2. It might be remarked, incidentally, that transformation is a striking recurrent motif in narratives throughout the archipelago and appears in tales of various genres.

gills. This was why he was ill and could not eat. The owner had secreted a sharp stick, which he used for tapping the palm wine, in his sarong and he asked the king to shut his eyes and for everyone else leave the room. He removed the hook and the king recovered his health. Before returning home the king presented the fisherman with a necklace with twelve strands, among other things, and told him that when he returned home he was to place these objects outside his house and under some leaves and to wait until the following morning when he would find many buffaloes. The fisherman did not believe him, though, and after he had emerged from the spring he took only a few of the items and left the remainder. Next morning he found buffaloes everywhere. He searched diligently for the objects he had left behind but could not find them. Nor could he enter the spring.

Narrative 5

This story comes from the Kei islands and was published by Heinrich Gottfried Langen (1902: 55–57). It is less explicit than the majority of 'impalement' narratives discussed here, even to the point that one might claim that it is too marginal to be included in our set.[13] However, as I shall argue below, the motifs that it resorts to serve as sufficient justification for its inclusion within the set.

There were three brothers, Hian (the eldest), Tongiil, and Papara. Papara went fishing in the cloud-sea and lost his elder brother's fishing rod. Hian became very angry and ordered Papara to go in search of it. Papara dived down into the clouds. There he encountered a fish called Kaliboban who asked him what he was looking for. Papara told him the truth. He explained what had happened. Kaliboban promised to find the missing fishing rod and he proved as good as his word because he found the fishing rod inside the mouth of another fish, whose name was Kerkeri, extracted it, and

---

13 I am indebted to Professor Guido Sprenger for making a copy of the original Langen text available to me and for Ms Katharina Stöhr who was so kind as to provide me with a translation of the narrative.

gave it to Papara. The story does not state that Papara actually returned the implement, but it does go on to state that Papara schemed to take 'revenge' on his eldest brother (apparently for being angry and ordering him to go on the quest). So one day as Hian lay sleeping Papara hung a bamboo tube, filled with palm wine, a very expensive commodity in what the narrative describes as 'heaven', on his brother's bed, in such a fashion that the tube would immediately drop and spill the palm wine as soon as Hian got up. This occurred and Papara ordered Hian to fetch some palm wine to refill the container. Hian commenced his search by digging a hole in the sky in an excavation that reached the earth. But Hian did not find any palm wine.[14]

In this story the impalement motif is absent; the fraternal group consists of three brothers, not two; and the fraternal trio resides in the sky rather than on the land. Nor is an instrument of impalement as such mentioned; instead, it is a fishing rod that has ensnared the victim. Life and plenty are not included as a motif; clouds instead of water constitute the medium that mediates between the two worlds; and the contrast visible/invisible is absent. Despite these deviations from our pattern, I think the tale can just about be said to qualify for inclusion. Water appears in the form of clouds (cf. Narrative 3); the male sibling relationship in the context of the loss of the fishing rod involves the elder brother, and since in the sequence of named brothers the actions of the brother listed in the ultimate narrational position, Papara, are consistent with those of the younger brothers described in the other tales, one is justified in so identifying him. The motif of the elder brother/younger brother can plausibly be said to be present and the lost fishing hook replaced by its metonym, the fishing rod, while the motif of the quest appears, as does that of

---

14 The narrative continues to relate how the brothers, their sister, and their four dogs descended to earth. The failure of the elder brother to redress a mistake he makes recalls the failure of the eldest brother, Kemala, in Narrative 2, to successfully fulfil his obligation of restoring the sesame seeds to the golden tray.

deception. The status relationship reversal of the elder and younger brother occurs again.

Narrative 6

This narrative, which explains the origins of those members of the Makassai ethno-linguistic group living in the fishing settlement of Laga-Soba, ten kilometers east of Baucau Town in Timor-Leste,[15] is more opaque than the other stories presented here (Spillet 1999: 277–80). It includes the motif of the fishing hook, the line ('rope'), the deceitful protagonist (whose name is Bertiti), and an ailing fish. But we are not informed whether the protagonist even cures the invalid, and in any case he goes unrewarded. Even more unexpected, we are not informed whose fishing hook impales the victim. The protagonist hits his wife with an arrow, not the victim whom he eventually cures, i.e., his mother-in-law. Furthermore, he is not described as having any brothers and he is the husband of a fish.

One day Bertiti shot an arrow at a fish and accidently shot his wife in the ribs. She fled home to her parents. Bertiti went into the sea to search for his missing arrow and there met a crocodile[16] whom he tried to deceive by pretending that he was not on a quest. The crocodile, however, was well aware of what had occurred. The creature told Bertiti that his wife had taken the arrow back with her to her parents' home and that the artefact was on a shelf [presumably in her parents' house]. Bertiti sat on the crocodile's back and they dived below the sea to the wife's residence. Bertiti discovered that his mother-in-law was ill and despite the ministrations of the local doctor and the application of all their medicines the inhabitants of the underwater world had been unable to cure

15 In addition to the Baucau sub-district, the Makassai are found further west in the sub-district of Viqueque.

16 In Southeast Asian literature crocodiles are often thought of as having a kingly status and classed as predators endowed with the capacity – like eels and turtles – to transverse boundaries, such as the sea, or separating the underwater world from the world above. I am indebted to a reviewer for suggesting I include this observation.

her. After his wife had confided the problem to him, Bertiti went into the room where the woman lay ill and said that it were better if everyone left the invalid and himself alone in the room together. Bertiti had understood the sickness as being caused by a fishing hook impaling the woman's mouth and [for some unstated reason] took a piece of rope and tied it to her neck and began to try to remove the hook. But when he left the room to pass the rope to the people [perhaps so they could help him extract it] he realized that it was the rope and not the hook that was in his mother-in-law's mouth. Eventually, Bertiti climbed on the crocodile's back and went to Laga where he founded [i.e., gave life to] the social group that looks upon this narrative as their narrative of origin. The crocodile, who is the enabler for Bertiti as well as performing the function of being a mediator between the animistic world and the world of matter, became his group's[17] 'grandfather'.

Narrative 7

This narrative was collected among the Meto people of western Timor by P. Middelkoop (1958: 401–2).[18]

A man called But Ba'u was fishing with a fishing hook belonging to a man called Ome. A crocodile came along and swallowed it, taking it with him into the sea. Learning what had occurred Ome became very angry and told But Ba'u that he must go in search of it. But Ba'u could not find the hook. Then he spied a turtle on the seashore who inquired what he was looking for. But Ba'u replied that he was merely going to and fro. The turtle was not deceived. He said that But Ba'u shouldn't just go hither and yon: the crocodile-king's body was 'badly hurt'. But Ba'u climbed on top of the turtle's back and the creature ordered him to close

17 Most likely, this group is a clan and the crocodile its totemic culture hero.

18 Middlekoop includes another text featuring a fishing hook and the protagonist, But Ba'u, who together with a turtle undertakes a sea voyage to the realm of a king. However, the sibling relationship is absent and the combination of motifs that give the story its integrity places it outside the genre considered here.

his eyes. 'Suddenly' they arrived at the palace of the king, whom they found sleeping. The turtle awoke the king and called to But Ba'u, who saw the king's wide-open 'beak' and the fishing hook. He took a twig of *kusambi* (*Schleichera oleosa*) and told those present to close their eyes. He retrieved the fishing hook, which he had hidden, and said: 'Open your eyes.' When those present had opened their eyes they saw that their king had recovered. But Ba'u displayed the twig, which he had moistened with his tongue and was red all over [presumably indicative of blood]. The king wished to pay him but But Ba'u refused because of orders that the turtle had given, and although the king kept importuning him But Ba'u kept declining. The king finally said: 'This man has bewitched me to kill me, we want to pay him, but he refused me once and for all.' Those present tried to find a way to kill But Ba'u but the turtle took him on his back and fled with him and brought him up to his 'ceiling' [presumably the surface of the sea]. The turtle gave But Ba'u four papayas and told him that when he arrived ashore he was to place the papayas on the edge of a pool he would find there and that after four nights should come and look 'after them'. But Ba'u did so and then returned the fishing hook to Ome. Four nights passed. He went to see the papayas and found four buffaloes in the pool together with the turtle who told him to go home and return after a further four nights. Four nights later he discovered eight buffaloes in the pool. He 'drove them up' from the water in the pool and took them home. Out hunting later, Ome discovered But Ba'u milking buffaloes. Ome's dog spilt But Ba'u's milk. But Ba'u became very angry and told Ome he must replace his milk because when he had lost his fishing hook Ome had been furious with him and that he had forced But Ba'u to go searching for the missing fishing hook until he found it. Accordingly, But Ba'u told Ome that because he had spilt the milk he must dig into the ground and that if he found the milk it would be Ome's; but if he found water it would be But Ba'u's. Ome found water, and so it belonged to But Ba'u.

MOTIFS

Table 1 illustrates the frequency with which the seven motifs occur in these seven narratives and it shows that five of these motifs occur in every text: water, life and plentitude, the fishing hook or its various surrogates, the quest, and the deception/error motif.

Visible/Invisible

The alternation between the opening of the eyes and closing of the eyes is a motif commonly occurring in eastern Indonesian narratives. Closing the eyes serves as a marker indicating escape from the confines of the material world to the spiritual world and return from the spiritual world back to the material world. Opening the eyes indicates entrance into the opposite ontological domain. The condition with eyes closed corresponds to the period during which the protagonist in the tale is in a state of liminality engaged on a journey of greater or lesser duration. He/she is neither in the material world nor in that of the animistic world. As such, and as established earlier, closing the eyes corresponds to the rites of separation, while opening of the eyes corresponds to the rites of integration. Another situation in which the act of closing the eyes occurs is when a protagonist is engaging in an act of deception.

The opening/closing of the eyes serves, in addition, to convey the contrast between visibility/invisibility.[19] In the world of matter the protagonist closes his eyes and it becomes invisible to him. While they are closed he remains enclosed in a transient condition or stage of liminality; when he opens his eyes he finds that he is in the domain of spirit. Later, he closes his eyes again, and the animistic world vanishes; the liminal stage returns; finally, upon re-opening his eyes he once again confronts the material world. In Narrative 3 the spiritual domain is visible to Bui but invisible to her mother and all prospects

---

19 I am grateful to Professor Guido Sprenger (personal communication) for pointing out how the visible/invisible motif rather than that of opening eye/closing eye might help emphasize the continuity of the set of narratives analysed here.

Table 1 Motif occurrence frequency

Motifs	One	Two	Three	Four	Five	Six	Seven	Frequency
			Narratives					
Water	√	√	√	√	√	√	√	7
Life and Plenitude	√	√	√	√	–	√	√	6
Instrument of Impalement	√	√	√	√	–	√	√	6
The Quest	√	√	√	√	√	√	√	7
Deception/error	√	√	√	√	√	√	√	7
eB/yBr	√	√	–	–	√	√	√	5
Visible/Invisible	√	√	–	√	–	–	√	4

of it ever being visible to her vanish owing to her plucking out her grandchild's eye. Unlike the other instances of visibility/invisibility, which are temporary, this is a permanent condition of invisibility: both child and Bui remain invisible to human beings. By contrast, within the world of the spirit the motif of visible/invisible is resorted to in two distinct situations: (a) When the protagonist asks the attendants to first close and then open their eyes (Narrative 7), and (b) when he asks them to go out of the king's room and remain outside the victim's room (Narrative 4 and Narrative 6).

Elder Brother/Younger Brother

By now it should have become apparent that the motif of elder brother/younger brother is widespread in eastern Indonesia and in some narratives their relationship hinges on the motif of the fishing hook. It should not have escaped notice, either, that Narratives 3, 6, and 7 appear to lack it. In the first two stories the affinal relationship replaces, to some degree, that of the fraternal relationship. In Narrative 7, the respective protagonists are simply referred to as 'the man But Ba'u' and 'the man Ome'. In Chapter 6, I noted this anomaly and remarked that the plot in this story 'apparently' excluded this particular relationship. However, situating this narrative within the context of a semantic set whose definition includes interactions between elder brother and younger brother that demonstrably accord with similar actions in the other tales, we are able to infer that this story, in fact, describes yet another adventure of these two siblings (cf. Lévi-Strauss 1978: 25–33). Ome owns the fishing hook; But Ba'u loses it; Ome orders But Ba'u to recover it; But Ba'u, the socially inferior, succeeds, and after being transformed by his interaction with the spirits in an aquatic realm ends up with a very desirable material bounty Ome lacks. Ome's failure to rectify his mistake – made by his canine surrogate – obtains for But Ba'u the ownership of the most precious valuable, water, and denies it to Ome. The spilling of milk in this tale and its irretrievable mixing into the earth replicates in a slightly different way the the incident in which the elder brother in Narrative 2 spills his younger brother's sesame seeds into the earth and is unable to retrieve them. In both cases whereas the previously subordinate younger brother succeeds in his mission, the erstwhile superordinate elder brother fails. In his article Prager (p. 450) remarks the relevance for Narrative 2 of the common theme of 'stranger outsider', famously identified, as was mentioned earlier in this book, in its Austronesian context by Marshal Sahlins (1985). This is given expression to in various ways, among them narratives in which the younger brother travels or is transported to the spiritual world and upon his return finds himself assuming the office of king (Hicks 1988: 812–13). In the above set of stories the same sort of transformation occurs in the younger brother's role in society. From his native space he travels to an alien world and comes back transformed by his encounter with the spirits and affects changes in his old world. His native context may also be interpreted as the inner or interior world and his transient destination as the outer or exterior world, another common Indonesian dualism, and one discernible among the Tetum-speaking peoples of Timor (Hicks 1984: *passim*).[20]

Deception/Error

The motif of the successful deception or error plays a pivotal role in the plots in which it appears, for had the ploy failed the narrative

---

20 I thank Professor Guido Sprenger for reminding me of this analogy.

would have had a radically different outcome. In Narrative 1 the protagonist requests as his reward what seems a trifle, but this humble gift transforms itself into (literally) gold and in Narrative 2 the younger brother devises a trap into which his elder brother falls. In Narratives 4, 6, and 7 the younger brother deceives the deity who fails to realize the younger brother's culpability in causing his injury. In Narratives 2, 5 and 6 the mistake made inverts the status relationship between the erstwhile superordinate elder brother and his erstwhile subordinate junior. Two plots make use of what might be called 'negative' deception in the sense that the attempt at deception fails. In Narrative 6 the crocodile is not deceived by Bertiti and in Narrative 7 the turtle is not deceived by But Ba'u.

The Quest

In three of the tales the quest involves a journey undertaken by a younger brother into the animistic world followed by his successful return (see Hicks 1988). In these narratives a protagonist undertakes a quest to fulfil an obligation and returns – the cycle completed, duty to his social superior discharged, and freely-given life-sustaining help rendered a deity – with benefits accruing to himself. In Narrative 3, however, an unmarried girl in her capacity as an intended bride for the deity travels to the spiritual domain where she marries him, provides the source of life for his descendants, and eventually remains in the realm of the spirit. In all the narratives male and female protagonists provide the means by which human beings obtain life and plentitude.

Instrument of Impalement

The motif of the instrument of impalement, whether in its most characteristic form, the fishing hook, or one of its surrogates, serves as a cultural device for 'hooking', as it were, the world of matter into that of the spirit and securing the benefits that accrue from their reciprocal relationship. Enhanced by the support of the other motifs, this is accomplished within the natural medium of water that thereby acts as the procreative agency that makes life and plentitude possible.

Life and Plentitude

While we may assess Hocart's claim to lie somewhat on the hyperbolic side, the plangency of his prose emphasizes the extent to which the quest for life, fertility, and abundance in general – essential elements for human existence – finds aesthetic expression in action and – if only by implication – involves conjunction between two metaphysical existences. As in ritual, so too in narrative. Not only can life and plentitude be obtained by performance in the former; they can also be pursued in expository fashion in the latter. But whereas fertility rituals enact or bring about rapport between spirit and matter, narratives verbalize the experiences of those who entertain them and permit a glimpse into how people conceive their relationship with their animistic counterparts.

Water

In these stories water furnishes an environment conducive to the conjunction of spirit and matter and thereby facilitates their reciprocity. Although of a material nature, water, because it shares a proximate identity with the animistic domain, shows itself to possess a more ambivalent character, one consistent with its role as an agent of transformation. As an enabling agency, water is the natural correspondent of the fishing hook. An artefact of culture, and moreover one that is unambiguously of the material world, the fishing hook, by contrast, makes possible a fertile interaction with spirit by facilitating its 'capture'.

CONCLUSION

In the foregoing narratives the spirits victimized, as it were, by the hook of the predator from the material world, are water-dwellers that are harmless to human beings. All, that is, except for the victim in Narrative 7, who proves to be a crocodile. Hence, the protagonist in all the stories, except in that tale, accepts gifts from his victims whose sickness he has cured. To do so, however, when his gift-giver is a crocodile, would place him in a relationship created and sustained by an exchange of gifts with a creature every bit as much a predator as himself. To avoid placing himself in a gift-relationship that is balanced, and therefore equal, the human protagonist fends off the opportunity to establish a relationship with a fellow predator and spurns the gift offered by the crocodile. Not that he goes unrewarded, for the mediating turtle, which reconciles the worlds of the spiritual and material, provides him with his compensation. The human being's gift comes from a non-predator.

These seven narratives portray a pair of interdependent ontological domains mutually engaged in sustaining each other in a reciprocal relationship. Spirits require homage and food from human beings, while human beings, for their part, need life and plentitude, a dialectic described for other ethnographic regions including South America and North Asia.[21] In the imaginations of the peoples of the archipelago, therefore, I suggest that water may be construed as the aforementioned 'penumbra' of our epigraph, an ambiguous substance by whose very ambiguity 'the clear visibility of things material' and 'their total extinction in the spiritual' merge, as spirit envelops matter with the mystery of 'soul suggestion'.

This conclusion suggests a possible answer to one question that may be posed. It will not have escaped attention that all these narratives depict an alternative world inhabited by animals. Narrative 3 might be thought an exception, yet, although in that story the spirit (the god of the mountain) is intangible and invisible he becomes reified in material form as the boar.[22] The 'penumbra', as it were, consists of the underwater denizens themselves. The hero of these tales does not confront spirits as such. This penumbral quality raises an interesting issue of ontological classification when the deployment of animal imagery in these narratives of eastern Indonesia is compared with the ways in which societies in other ethnographic regions, such as South America and Northeast Asia, incorporate the world of animals into the respective domains of human beings and spirits (cf.

---

21 See Conklin (1995); Pederson (2010).
22 An observation I owe to Dr Rodemeier (Rodemeier 2013).

Århem 1996; Conklin 1995; Pederson 2001). Are these underwater animals, in fact, spirits, or creatures of the material world? Do these narratives depict three worlds (spiritual; animal; human) or only two (spiritual/material)? If the latter case, the material world itself would be binary: human/animal. According to this interpretation these seven tales describe a spiritual world and a material world, but the latter contains a human sub-world and an animal sub-world. The argument for regarding the animals as simply animals is clear, for there is nothing especially immaterial in their behaviour or in the environment in which they live, and the physical pain that the instrument of impalement inflicts on the creature implies a material affliction hardly consistent with an ontological mode of immateriality.

At the beginning of this chapter, I raised the question: 'How can the insubstantial engage with the substantial or how can invisible and intangible spirits be 'thought' into a relationship with visible and tangible human beings?' The foregoing analysis suggests a possible answer. If water, in these tales, is seen as an ambiguous medium that conjoins, indeed syncretically intermixes the material and spiritual, the ontological status of these underwater denizens becomes evident. These water animals possess the qualities of both spirit[23] and creature. They are, at one and the same time, spirits and animals, immaterial and spiritual, and visible and invisible. Fish are denizens of an opaque medium. They are present, yet invisible, to those outside, and therefore have the potential to serve as representations of an animal kingdom that might be conceived as a third mode of existence. The eel, for its part, provides a natural link between the worlds of the spirit and the realm of the material, as does the cultural device of the instrument of impalement.[24] By the process of alternatively closing

---

23 The inhabitants of the underwater world present themselves in such a way as to be described as spirits, as among the Nage, for example, who refer to them as *nitu*, a term denoting 'spirit', and the ethnographer, Gregory Forth (1998: 42), so designates them.

24 Like crocodiles and turtles, eels and snakes are, of course, in the literature of Southeast Asia, common mediators between the world of the spirit and the human realm. The previous chapter discussed a narrative from Caraubalo

and opening his eyes a human being, typically (as we have seen) a younger brother, can gain access to this other world and thereby empower himself sufficiently enough to engage with the source of life and plenitude. In collusion with the eyes, the instrument of impalement makes it possible for the human being to see what remains invisible to his fellows as he enters into an engagement with the third ontological domain. Water is the opaque or semi-opaque window[25] through which human beings may, on occasion, catch – even if only briefly – a vague glimpse of the undefined, penumbral, world that is the home of the spiritual entities that their imaginations, furnished by experience and knowledge of the world, have conceived. Through it, the mysterious can be almost caught sight of; and the imminence of the unknown becomes, if only for a brief moment, palpable.

REFERENCES

Anon. 1982. 'The Luck of the Sea and the Luck of the Mountains', in *The Kojiki: Records of Ancient Matters*. XXXIX–XLII. Translated by Basil Hall Chamberlain.

suku in which an eel, Ali-iku, part-human/part-deity, first of all appears in a stream as a cultural hero who founds a clan and then disappears into the depths of a stream, and in other Caraubalo narratives demons from the underworld appear as snakes in the material world and initiate an ambiguous relationship with human beings. In *A Maternal Religion* (1984: 96) I note that some psychoanalysts have suggested that the snake image mediates in the unconscious mind between this world and the other world (Henderson 1964:154–156) and interpreting Timorese symbolic thought in light of Endicott's suggestion (Endicott 1970: 136) about magical thinking among the Malays, I further argued that in Tetum culture, because water weakens the boundaries that keep categories discreet, it facilitates passage between different domains. To that earlier conclusion I would now add that water serves as an exemplary medium for establishing relationships between the human domain and that of the spirit domain.

25 'Water seems to weaken the boundaries between many kinds of category, facilitating passage across them. [...] Even spirits cross boundaries with the aid of water. [...] The quality that gives water the ability to weaken boundaries is probably its fluidity, the complete lack of 'hardness'. It will sustain no divisions or boundaries of its own' Endicott (1970: 136).

Århem Kaj 1996. 'The Cosmic Food-web: human–nature relatedness in the Northwest Amazon', in P. Descola and G. Pálsson (eds), *Nature and Society: Anthropological Perspectives*. London; New York: Routledge.

Bosch, F. D. K. 1960. *The Golden Germ: an introduction to Indian symbolism*. The Hague: Mouton.

Brooker, Christopher 2004. *The Seven Basic Plots: why we tell stories*. London and New York: Continuum.

Caffin, Charles 1910. *Camera Work*. New York: Alfred Stieglitz. Number 31, July.

Conklin, Beth A. 1995. ''Thus are Our Bodies, Thus was Our Custom': mortuary cannibalism in an Amazonian Society'. *American Ethnologist, Volume* 22: 75–201.

Endicott, Kirk 1970. *Malay Magic*. Oxford: Clarendon Press.

Forth, Gregory 1998. *Beneath the Volcano: religion, cosmology and spirit classification among the Nage of eastern Indonesia. Verhandelingen van het Koninklijk Instituut voor Taal-, Land- en Volkenkunde* 177. Leiden: KITLV Press.

Henderson, Joseph L. 1964. 'Ancient Myths and Modern Man', in Carl Jung & M. L. van Franz (eds), *Man and his Symbols*. New York: Garden City. Doubleday & Company, Inc.

Hicks, David 1984. *A Maternal Religion: the role of women in Tetum myth and ritual*. DeKalb: Northern Illinois University, Center for Southeast Asian Studies. Monograph Series on Southeast Asia. Special Report No. 22.

—— 1988. 'Literary Masks and Metaphysical Truths: intimations from Timor'. *American Anthropologist* 90 (4): 807–817.

—— 2007. 'Younger Brother and Fishing Hook on Timor: reassessing Mauss on hierarchy and divinity'. *Journal of the Royal Anthropological Institute (new series)* 13 (1): 39–56.

Hitchcock, Michael 1996. *Islam and Identity in Easter Indonesia*. Hull: The University of Hull Press.

Hocart, Arthur Maurice 1954. *Social Origins*. London: Watts & Company.

Langen, Heinrich Gottfried 1902. *Die Key-oder Kii-Inseln des O. I. Archipelago: aus dem Tagebuche eines Kolonisten.* Vienna.

Lévi-Strauss, Claude 1979. *Myth and Meaning: cracking the code of culture.* New York: Shocken Books.

Middlekoop, P. 1958. 'Four Tales with Mythical Features Characteristic of the Timorese People'. *Bijdragen toot de Taal-, Land- en Volkenkunde* 114: 384–405.

Palmer, Lisa n. d. Water Relations: Customary Systems and the Management of Baucau City's Water. Unpublished Ms.

—— 2010. Personal communication.

Pederson, Morten A. 2001. 'Totemism, Animism and North Asian Indigenous Ontologies', *Journal of the Royal Anthropological Institute (new series)* 3: 411–27.

Prager, Michael 2010. 'The Appropriation of the 'Stranger King': polarity and mediation in the Dynastic Myth of Bima'. In *The Anthropology of Values: essays in honour of Georg Pfeffer*, edited by Peter Berger, Roland Hardenberg, Ellen Kattner and Michael Prager. New Delhi: Pearson. Pp. 447–70.

—— 2011. Personal communication. 24th February.

Rodemeier, Susanne 2009. 'Bui Hangi – the Deity's Human Wife'. *Anthropos* 104: 469–482).

—— 2013. Personal communication, August 19.

Sahlins, Marshal 1985. 'The Stranger King; or Dumézil among the Historians', in *Islands of History*. Chicago: University of Chicago Press.

Spillet, P. G. 1999. *The Pre-Colonial History of the Island of Timor together with Some Notes on the Makassan Influence in the Island.* Darwin, Australia: Museum and Art Gallery of the Northern Territory.

Sprenger, Guido 2011. Personal communication. February 24.

Tylor, Edward 1873. *Primitive Culture,* Vol. 1. 2nd edition. London: John Murray, Albemarle Street.

CHAPTER 8

Exchange, Water, and Motif in an Etic Genre of Narrative

Exchange is a ubiquitous feature of all societies and my concern in this chapter is to demonstrate its function in the field of verbal narrative and describe how, in conjunction with water, reciprocal relationships find expression in a distinctive genre of Timorese oral literature.

For scholars concerned with verbal art, Timor-Leste offers a treasure trove of riches. Not only is there a diversity of genres, but within each genre there is also a rich variety of sub-genres. Although hundreds of oral narratives have been collected, principally by Portuguese missionaries, very few indeed have been analysed in any depth, notable exceptions occurring in the work of the Catholic missionaries Father Basílio da Sá (1961), Father Enes Pascoal (1967) and Father Jorge Duarte (n.d., 1984)[1] whose contributions were acknowledged in other chapters.

In Chapter 7, I sought to show how certain motifs or repetitive narrative segments in the oral and written literature of the archipelago combine and recombine in such a manner as to produce narratives with a consistent and distinct literary character. My intention in this final chapter is to offer further empirical collaboration for that argument. I shall do so by examining four narratives from Timor-Leste possessing this characteristic and add weight to my argument that the repetition of these motifs results in bringing about a distinctive category of narrative.[2]

---

1 Narratives are also to be found in other works.

2 I should like to thank Dr Susana Matos de Viegas and Dr Rui Graça Feijó for inviting me to give the keynote speech at the 'Dynamics: Land, Exchange, Governance. Timor-Leste in Context' International Conference held at the Museu do Oriente and Instituto Ciências Sociais, Lisbon, on 19–24

Bronislaw Malinowski famously drew attention to the importance of noting the verbal categories that indigenous societies employ in classifying narratives. In properly remarking the necessity for ethnographers to identify the indigenous taxonomy, Malinowski may have given the impression that what one might, following Marvin Harris, identify as an 'etic' classification, was a questionable usurpation of the local taxonomy. A subsidiary intention of this essay is to argue for the merits of an etic classification as a means of comprehending how Timorese narratives are, so to speak, assembled. In doing so I shall attempt to demonstrate how, in four narratives of a sub-genre that Lisa Palmer (2015: 27) calls 'water stories', make use of a theme. ubiquitous in Timorese narratives, to which attention has already been drawn on numerous occasions. This is the theme of transformation, and it implicates two opposing, yet complementary, domains that constitute Timorese cosmology; that of matter (*rai laran* in Tetum) and that of spirit (*rai seluk*). We shall see that this medium, both fresh or salt, operates as an agent enabling interactions between the human domain and the domain of the other world, i.e., of *mate bein, mate klamar*,[3] the *rai na'in, we na'in*, and the other spirits that inhabit it, and operates as an agent in facilitating transformations, some of which are ontological and others of which are social. I attempt to show that the plots, *dramatic personae*, and motifs of each of the four narratives resonate with those of the other three such that the corpus of tales presents itself as a set or 'suite' whose dominant motifs cohere such

---

January 2015, which provided this essay with its initial formal version. It was a privilege I was honoured and gratified to have received. Dr Viegas also provided me with valuable editorial suggestions. I am also grateful to Dr João Amorim, Director, *Vogal da Comissão Executiva, Fundação Oriente Museu*, for granting me a residence at the Foundation's magnificent centre in Dili for a period of six weeks to enable me to carry out my research. This essay is one product of his investment in my scholarly work. My gratitude, too, is extended to Mrs Graça Viegas, manager for making my residence as comfortable as it was productive. Again my thanks go to Dr Susana de Matos Viegas, this time for the critical part that she played in making my residence possible.

3   Souls of the recently deceased.

as to bind them into a 'set' in the sense recognized by Claude Lévi-Strauss (1979). Not all the six motifs considered here are necessarily deployed to the same degree in each narrative, but they recur frequently enough to impart unity to the entire set. The aforementioned motifs, to which I have already drawn attention (Chapter 7), may be summarized as (a) a quest, sometimes in response to a command, that results in fulfilment of some sort; (b) an inappropriate action, typically a deception or ruse, a violation of some prohibition or convention, or error; (c) an alternation between the invisible and visible, typically signaled by the shutting and closing of the eyes; (d) life, health, and abundance; (e) a status reversal, either of a cosmic or social character; and (f) an artefact of impairment, typically a fishing hook, machete, or arrow.[4] Scholars of Timorese ethnography are familiar with narratives that sporadically introduce these narrative segments, for they are common in Timorese tales, and Susana Barnes (2011: 27–28), to give just one instance, records a narrative in which, among two brothers, the elder commits an infringement of a taboo regarding their common sacred (*lulik*) land and other *sacra*, an action that disrupts and transforms, their relationship. But in the narrative set that concerns us here this motif of an inappropriate action is a recurrent companion of its five partners. Complementing these six motifs are others that are commonplace in Timorese oral narrative: hierarchy, agnation, exchange, and affinity.

My procedure is as follows. After a few words by way of introduction I give the plots of each narrative, providing each with its provenance and adding comments relevant to the six motifs. I then discuss the motifs in more detail and conclude by considering the role of water in Timorese symbolism, for it is this medium that provides the cosmological context for the operation of these motifs.

Given the desiccated nature of the eastern region of the Malaysian Archipelago it is not surprising that water should come to occupy a prominent place in many tales told in this region. In all these narratives water is the context which makes possible mediation or

---

4   As in Bunak narratives (Sousa, personal communication, 2015).

connectivity between the material and the spiritual and serves as an enabler for relationships of exchange in which benefits, most commonly life, health, fertility, abundance, and social status accrue to at least one of the tales' protagonists. In these works of the Timorese imagination, the instrument of impairment is frequently the property of a socially superior person, typically an elder brother, whose social inferior, after losing the artefact, engages in a quest to retrieve it, the outcome of the quest inverting the terms of their relative statuses in the pre-existing hierarchy.

In these tales the human protagonist interacts with figures from a world that is 'set apart' – as Durkheim claimed for his concept of 'the sacred' – from the ordinary world of the secular or material. This world is frequently located underwater, but in some tales is an island or some other alien territory. Whatever its location, however, a fluvial divide separates it from the mundane world that human beings inhabit and its denizens are not the kind you expect to meet in everyday village society. They include eels that are younger brothers, crocodiles and fish that are kings, and turtles that provide transportation for human beings. In the previous chapter and in Hicks (2016) I suggested that these apparent animals are, in fact, manifestations of spirit, an identification finding support in the work of Gregory Forth (1998: 42) who notes, as we saw in the previous chapter, that among the Nage, of Flores, such underwater 'creatures' are known as *nitu*, a term denoting 'spirit'. And, as Judith Bovensiepen (2011: 50) has described for the Idate-speaking peoples of Funar in Laclubar, a certain ambiguity exists regarding the exact nature of the relationship between the *mate bein* and the *rai na'in*. *Lulik* she sees as being closely connected here with these spiritual entities which, she remarks, although conceptually separate, are nevertheless ritually 'implicitly treated as transformations of each other and their combined potency in the land makes up its powerful potency'. If these underwater denizens are indeed transformations of these spirits I would propose that, in certain cases, the denizens of the water are transformations of that category of spiritual entity common throughout Timor-Leste known as *we na'in*, a local *genius loci*, whose terrestrial counterpart is the *rai*

160

na'in. In that it is the realm of spirit, this world is also the realm of the *mate bein*, ancestors who, from the dead, summon up the means of life, health, fertility and exchange them with their living human kin. As Palmer (2015: 90) puts it, water, in the form of 'spring water, [is] a substance which connects the world of the living with that of the dead'. Springs, in particular, function as a threshold for exchange and reciprocity between the visible and invisible worlds. Yet it is not only spring water that functions as the connector: all manner of aquatic sources – rivers, streams, the sea – do so as well; as, of course, does the water employed in ritual.

Despite the fact that water is the theme that connects in a Lévi-Staussian manner the narratives discussed here, exchange constitutes the formal transformative device that connects the worlds of the ancestors and living human beings.[5] in certain of the tales discussed here this device is readily apparent but sometimes – as in the case of the narrative that begins this series of narratives, it is more implicit than explicit.

THE NARRATIVES

Narrative 1: The Story of the Eel Clan

I commence with a narrative that I collected from the *suku* of Caraubalo in Viqueque sub-district in the Tetum language during my first period of research in 1966 (see Chapter 8, fn. 12 and Hicks 1984: 27) and 're-collected' during a later period of field research.[6] Among other things, it accounts for the origins of a local clan called Eel.

> One day seven brothers went for a walk. At midday they ordered their youngest brother, whose name was Ali-iku, to collect water from a nearby stream. In the middle of the stream was an eel making the water muddy, so the youngest brother returned empty handed to tell his elder brothers what he had seen. They disbelieved his story and commanded him to return. The water was

5   An insight I owe to Dr Susana Matos de Viegas.
6   In 2005.

still dirty though and he was unable to get any. The eldest brother, armed with his machete, returned with the youngest brother. The eldest brother lifted up the eel and hacked it to death. They then collected water and carried it back with the eel to their brothers. The elder brothers ordered the youngest brother to cook it while they went for a stroll. As the eel cooked it spoke to the youngest, telling him that when the sun set they two would be of the same flesh. The youngest brother ran to tell his elder brothers, and they came to listen, but the words had stopped. So the elder brothers disbelieved him, and resumed their walking. The eel repeated his words twice but the brothers continued to disbelieve the youngest brother. They returned to eat the meal that the youngest brother had prepared. The cooked rice and eel meat were divided in such a manner that the six had fully cooked rice and meat, but, though his rice was cooked, the youngest brother's piece of meat was still raw. After the meat was eaten they went to wash and frolic in the spring, and when the time came for them to leave, the six elder brothers climbed out of the water, but the youngest brother (who was now an Eel) could not, for while his head was still that of a human being, his body was an eel's. Calling the six brothers to him, he said: 'Today I told you what I had seen, but you refused to believe me. Now do you see? Yet don't feel sorry for me. Go! Purchase a red pig! Bring it here with some red rice. Roast this pig and cook the red rice.' After they had obeyed his commands he ordered them to place their portions on a plate and his on a banana leaf. On a wide stone covered with a palm leaf they placed both rice and meat. This done, they ate, and afterward listened to his instructions which were that henceforth they and their descendants must not eat certain foods, including eel meat; none be named after the eldest brother; and none bathe in that stream. He taught them songs and dances, and after doing so beat his head against a rock, and completed his full transformation into an eel. He then left and the brothers split up, three travelling to the west and three to the east. The eldest brother travelled east and settled down in a place called 'Uma Fatin', which means 'The Place of the

House [i.e., clan]'. His descendants founded the three lineages that today form the Eel clan.

This narrative describes how the Eel clan was founded and identifies its founder as a visitant from the domain of the spirit that proved to be a transient human being, the youngest of a group of brothers. The tale is one of birth and life and the hero is ambiguous. He is partly human and partly spirit; initially a social inferior who is under a social obligation to defer to his senior brothers or brothers and whose position in the social hierarchy is subsequently inverted and who is transformed into a founding creator of a descent group. Death is also present, for the younger brother is sacrificed as part of the process of creation. This sacrifice is agnatic in its nature, but – in contrast to the other narratives – bridewealth is absent from the story and there is no mention of women. The artefact of impairment is a machete; the error is committed by the eldest brother in cutting up the eel-spirit; and the initially visible and material youngest brother becomes invisible (presumably by submerging himself under the water) and is transformed into a spirit. There is a parallel here with the narratives told by Makassai and Wai Ma' residing along the Viqueque-Baucau Corridor, about whom Lisa Palmer (2015: 72) writes: 'In some accounts, particular named eels and civet cats are the founding ancestors of particular sacred houses. Similarly, as we will see below, both these eels and spring water are believed to have been able, at least in the distant past, to completely shift location by emerging from the ground and changing into human form. These newly transformed family groupings would then travel across the landscape to relocate to a new site before morphing back into the land as eels and spring water.'

The youngest brother in his capacity as the divine founder of the eel clan confers the gift of culture on his elder brothers and in return would appear to receive nothing. But in fact the latter willingly invert their status *vis-a-vis* their youngest brother when they accept his orders and instructions. A variation of this origin narrative occurs in a Nauete narrative recorded by Susana Barnes (2017: 74–85). It describes a journey undertaken by seven brothers to find fertile land, an endeavour in which they are assisted by a sacred crocodile-king. The brothers do not know how to cultivate the soil when they arrive at a fertile region but the youngest brother, offering himself up as a sacrifice for the benefit of his brothers, is killed by his eldest brother and is the agency by which his agnates acquire this knowledge. In sacrificing his life to benefit his brothers a cycle of exchange is formed between the living and their ancestors.

Narrative 2: Princess Nai Lou Becomes Ill

This narrative comes from Samoro, a Tetum-speaking region in the south-central area of Timor-Leste and was collected by Father Artur Basílio de Sá (1961: 45–65).[7]

> An elder brother and his younger brother enjoyed sea-fishing together. One day, however, the elder brother remained home and so his younger brother asked his brother's wife to loan him his brother's fishing hook to fish. She handed it over, but cautioned him not to lose the hook because otherwise her husband would be angry. The younger brother went off to fish. A big fish snatched up the hook, severed the line and escaped with the hook in its mouth. This fish was actually the only daughter of a king who ruled over an island. Returning home the younger brother offered his brother his own hook in replacement, but the angry elder brother refused the substitute. He ordered the junior man to go and find it. To start his quest the younger brother cast a fishing-net into the sea, threw himself on it and was borne along the surface until he came to the island over which the king ruled. There he met two young women who told him that the local populace was grieving on account of the fact that their princess had been stricken ill. None could cure her. As soon as the younger brother learned that the pain was located in the princess's throat he inferred what the cause might be and told them that he knew of a cure but would not say what it was. Along the way, as the girls were taking the younger brother through the woods to see the princess, they passed a bamboo grove and he sliced

---

7   See Chapter 6 and Hicks (2007: 45–46).

off a hook-shaped sliver of bamboo. When the younger brother saw the princess he said that her eyes should be covered and that he must be left alone with her. He was obeyed and was able to confirm his diagnosis: his hook was indeed lodged in the throat. Carefully extracting the artefact, he substituted for it the bamboo sliver. The younger brother called everyone to see the bamboo hook, the sight of which astounded them, and they declared that the young man had saved the princess's life. The younger brother asked the king for permission to leave the island, but the latter urged him to remain a while. The king asked his subjects how best to reward the young man and they told him that since he was growing old and there was no man to look after the kingdom, he should give their unexpected benefactor his daughter's hand in marriage and make him king. The king made this proposal to the younger brother who agreed but asked that he be allowed to return for a time to the mainland to see his elder brother. Using the net, as before, he returned to his elder brother's house and delivered the hook. After a short stay the younger brother went back to the sea, threw out his net, and went back to the palace. There the two youngsters married and the king handed the government of the realm over to them.

All six motifs occur here. We also have transformation (the younger brother becomes a king), exchange (the younger brother revivifies the crocodile's ailing daughter while the crocodile gives him his daughter's hand in marriage); agnation (the father–daughter relationship); and affinity (the crocodile becomes wife-giver to the younger brother), which confers upon him precedence in the ontological hierarchy. The motif of visibility/invisibility is manifested, not by the eyes, but by a blanket being placed as a cover over the daughter's eyes.

Narrative 3: The Sacred Spring of Corluli

This narrative is either Tetum or Ema and was collected by Father Jorge Duarte (n.d.).[8]

---

8   See Chapter 5. I wish to pay tribute to the late Father Duarte for generously placing the original manuscript containing this text at my disposal; in his

A man of royal lineage had a daughter and two sons. One day, while his elder brother was gardening, the younger brother took the elder brother's fishing hook and went to fish at a spring locally considered sacred. A crocodile seized the fishing hook, which stuck in its throat and was torn from the fishing line. The elder brother demanded compensation.[9] Now it happened that the younger brother grew betel in his garden and sometime after he lost the hook he found some of his betel leaves had been stolen and discovered that a cockatoo-woman was the thief. The cockatoo-woman explained that she was collecting them to cure her grandfather, a crocodile, who had sustained a mysterious injury. The younger brother inquired about the wound and learned the injury was in the crocodile's throat. When he told the cockatoo-woman he might be able to cure the grandfather's wound she invited him to accompany her to attempt a cure. The younger brother cut a piece of palm-leaf that had spines attached and hid it in a fold in his sarong. When they were ready to leave, the cockatoo-woman instructed him to close his eyes, which he did, and when he opened them he found himself already in her house where he saw the ailing crocodile languishing on the ground. The man ordered everyone in the room to leave and told the crocodile to close his eyes. Immediately he had done this, the younger brother extracted the hook from its mouth, hid it in his sarong, and by the time the crocodile opened his eyes the man was able to produce the piece of spiny palm-leaf and declare this object was what had caused the injury. The crocodile asked him what he wanted as a reward and the younger brother replied that he wished for a buffalo herd. The crocodile told him to build a corral. When the younger brother had done as he had been told the crocodile ordered him to close and open his eyes seven times. Each time he did so buffaloes appeared and kept appearing until the herd completely filled the corral. Then the crocodile himself made a request of the younger brother.

---

words, 'Any way you like'. My copy is dated 21 July 1989, and the narrative was told to Father Duarte by Francisco, the sexton in the Motael Church, Dili.

9   But does not oblige his younger brother to undertake a quest.

He desired a woman. The young man offered him a slave, but the crocodile preferred a princess of the same blood as the young man, and so the younger brother gave the crocodile his sister as a wife.

All six motifs occur in this tale, as does exchange (the younger brother revivifies the ailing crocodile while the crocodile reciprocates with a herd of buffaloes); agnation (the cockatoo-woman's father is a crocodile); and affinity (the younger brother gives the crocodile his sister in marriage and this wife-giving/wife-taking exchange elevates the human being over the crocodile-spirit.)

Narrative 4: Bemalai

This narrative comes from either the Tetum or Ema ethno-linguistic groups living in the region of Atabae (Pascoal 1967: 132–137).[10]

A husband and wife lived near the lagoon of Bemalai and had seven children. Six of them laboured daily in their gardens but the youngest son preferred to enjoy himself by hunting. Every day, after hunting, he would rub the soil over his body and onto his machete and pretend to his parents that he, too, had been busily at work. Suspecting deceit of some kind, his father spied on him one day and saw his most junior son hunting. That night the lad's mother put excrement on his plate as punishment. Furious, he went off to live by himself. In his new location the youngest brother made a garden in which he grew areca and betel. In time he married. He also fished in the sea. One day he impaled an unusually heavy fish on his hook and it broke the line. He was most unhappy, but to make things worse the following day he discovered that someone was stealing areca and betel from his garden. So the next night he lay in watch for the thief. Around dawn he noticed a cockatoo fly into the garden, where it transformed itself into a man, then helped himself freely to all the areca and betel he wanted. When confronted, the cockatoo-man explained he was stealing on behalf of his queen who was seriously wounded, and that the areca and

---

10 See Chapters 4 and 5.

betel were only medicines to cure her. The youngest brother did not believe him, so the cockatoo-man offered to take him to the queen's palace. They went to the beach, where the cockatoo-man told the youngest brother to close his eyes. Moments later he told him to open them. The youngest brother miraculously found himself in the palace and then verified what he had begun to suspect: that his hook was the culprit. He announced that he could cure the queen but needed to go into the forest to think about a remedy. Upon returning, the youngest brother said that he must consult alone with the patient, otherwise the remedy would fail. When the queen's attendants had gone he pulled out the hook so skilfully that not even the queen herself saw exactly what he had done, and when the attendants returned he held up a thorn he had taken from a palm tree when he was alone in the forest. This, he claimed, was what had caused the queen's pain. As a reward the queen told the youngest brother to return home and there make seven corrals. She instructed him to construct them so that the latest one was more spacious than its predecessor, thus making the seventh the largest. The man then found himself on the beach by the same miraculous process that had originally carried him to the queen's palace. He went home to work strenuously building the corrals. When the youngest brother had finished he went to the beach, where he found awaiting him the cockatoo-man, who told him to close and open his eyes. In an instant he found himself again before the queen, who said that, among other things, he should leave the entrance of each corral wide open, promising that countless buffaloes would soon appear. The youngest brother returned home in what was by now his customary manner to carry out his orders. At dawn the buffaloes began entering the corrals and continued doing so for many hours until all the buffaloes were inside the corrals, which then closed by themselves. In the entire region no one was as rich as this youngest brother. Because of this his brothers went to find him. They forced him to give them all the buffaloes because they were his elder brothers and the youngest brother was obligated to give them up. The youngest brother decided to complain to his benefactors and made his way back to the beach. With the help of the cockatoo-man and after opening and closing his eyes he found himself in the king's palace. Informed of the extortion the king told him to construct an outrigger canoe, hide it when it was ready so that no one would see it come and let him know. The youngest brother did as he was told and returned to inform the king with the help of the cockatoo-man. He didn't return to his house as on other occasions because the next day, following instructions he went to a sacred spring near the town of Maliana – as part of the retinue of the queen, who would go there because that was where her eldest child lived. At dawn everyone went to the beach where they transformed themselves into crocodiles, except for the youngest brother who was carried by the order of the queen to the sacred spring and hence to meet the queen's eldest son who lived nearby. The queen ordered the youngest brother to look at her son and then bring his daughter because she wished the two to be married. Reading reluctance in the man's face, the queen suspected a deception of some kind, and so she added that should the girl be his daughter, upon sensing her presence the water in the spring would rise up in clusters of spume. Otherwise the waters would remain tranquil. After opening and closing his eyes the youngest brother found himself back home where he told his wife what the queen had instructed. She refused to agree to the marriage so they dressed up their maid with pendants, bracelets of silver and gold, and, hanging from her neck and across her chest, rich, handsome necklaces. Combs made of silver, enhanced her hair, which was as black as ebony. Her skirt was the work of skilful weavers. Upon seeing her thus, thought the wife, even the waters of the sacred spring would be deceived. The queen received the maid with pleasure but no watery spume arose from the spring. The queen admonished the youngest brother for his deception and said to him: 'Return and if you don't bring your daughter your quarrel with your brothers will not be attended to.' Despite his wife, the youngest brother had to escort his daughter and they arrived at the spring. When the girl touched the water the young couple disappeared into the spring and no one ever saw them again.[11] The queen now told the youngest brother he should take ownership of a gourd full of water endowed with power. He received it respectfully and carried it to his brothers' village. The brothers were surprised to see him coming and were astonished when, showing them the water, the youngest brother said: 'From this day forth, even at the height of the summer, there will never be an absence of water because a great and new lake, which will never become dry, is going to appear. But first you must prepare a festival in which everybody takes part and which must last for seven days and seven nights.' When everyone was preoccupied with dancing, listening to the music, and drinking heavily the youngest brother carried his outrigger to an *uma lulik* and erected a cross at its centre. He hung the gourd from one of its cross-pieces and from the other he hung bones of buffaloes slaughtered at the festival. The festival reached its climax on the seventh night. As the youngest brother had anticipated, local dogs hurled themselves at the bones causing the gourd to fall and completely empty itself of the water. Together with his wife and the only brother who had not done anything bad to him, the youngest brother jumped into the outrigger. Almost everyone else perished in the waters.

Like Narrative 3, this narrative is one of a number of tales associated with the Bemalai lagoon. Although it lacks the quest for a missing fishing hook demanded by an elder brother, a younger brother does go on a quest, to discover if the cockatoo-man was speaking the truth about the impaired fish-queen, and it is the instrument that inspires his journey. The motif of an inappropriate action is amply expressed in the failure of the youngest brother to carry out his duty to cooperate with his siblings, his lies about working, the excrement being placed on his plate, the separation of the brothers from their agnatic abode, and the counterfeit bride. The motif of visible/invisible is

---

11 There is an echo here with the narrative of Bui Hangi, recounted in Chapter 7, in which the human girl, given in marriage to a deity, disappears forever in a mountain spring (Rodemeier 2009).

also expressed on multiple occasions, by the closing/opening of the youngest brother's eyes. Life, health and abundance are also given full rein in the curing of the queen and the multitude of buffaloes that appears, life-giving incidents in the story that contrast with the lethal devastation that destroys the community and all but one of the hero's brothers.[12] There are several status reversals. After the youngest brother returns to the material world as the richest person in the region, his elder brothers blatantly exploit their superior status in the social hierarchy by obliging him to relinquish his prize, but by the end of the story all but one have been killed by the younger brother's acting in concert with the underwater spirits. The spirit fish is first rendered sick (accidentally) by the youngest brother then cured by him but reciprocates with the gift of buffaloes and then enables the younger brother to obtain revenge and regain his buffaloes. The alternation of superiority/inferiority, expressed in this series of exchanges ends in the asymmetric affinal alliance in which the representative of the spiritual world becomes wife-taker to a member of the material world.

THE SIX MOTIFS

Having considered and commented on the narratives I shall now examine the six motifs in more detail.

1. Visibility and Invisibility

Visibility and invisibility, indicated by the alternation between the opening of the eyes and closing of the eyes is a motif commonly occurring in narratives told in the archipelago. Among other things, closing the eyes signifies escaping from the confines of the material world to the unlimited visions of the spiritual world and from the spiritual world back to the material world as well as supporting an act of deception. Opening the eyes indicates entrance into the opposite domain. The condition of eyes-closure corresponds to the period

---

12 Cf. the death of the younger brother, who abandons the material world for that of the spirit, in Narrative 1.

during which the protagonist in the tale is in a state of liminality, engaged on a journey of greater or lesser duration. He is neither in the material world nor in that of the animistic world. The analogy with a rite of passage is clear enough. Closing the eyes corresponds to the initial stage of separation, opening the eyes to the final stage of integration, and the more protracted period of blindness corresponds to the liminal stage. We might also think of the closure of the eyes as an act of symbolic death and the opening of the eyes as indicating a return to life.

Occasions when this motif comes into play are: when the younger brother asks the ailing spirit or its attendants to close and open their eyes; causes the eyes of the spirit to be covered; and when he himself enters and leaves the spirit world. In Narrative 1, these moments of visibility and invisibility are temporary and the act of opening and closing the eyes is absent. But whereas the youngest brother is visible in the material world to his elder brothers before his transformation, he disappears from human sight for ever after the transformation has been completed. The same permanent disappearance occurs in Narrative 4, when the affianced couple disappear into the waters forever.

2. Status Reversal

Social status is a recurring factor in all these narratives and is subject to reversal. In Narrative 1 the interaction between the brothers involves an ontological transformation as well as one of precedence. The inferior (pending) spirit, the youngest brother, after his ultimate fulfilment as a spirit, attains a position of superiority over his erstwhile superior older brothers (who are unambiguously human) and in the narratives that entail the healing of a spirit the human being initially asserts his precedence by impairing the spirit and subsequently by curing him of the ailment he has inflicted upon the invalid, although the relationship is balanced out in Narrative 2 in which the spirit becomes wife-giver to the man.[13]

---

13 The importance of status is cogently attested to in a West Timor narrative (Middlekoop 1958: 401–402) in which the human protagonist who has restored vitality to a spirit crocodile refuses to accept a gift from it so as

3. An Inappropriate Action

The motif of an inappropriate action, commonly a successful deception or error, plays a pivotal role in the plots in which it appears, for
had the ploy failed, the narrative would have had a different outcome;
but in Narrative 4 the motif makes its appearance as a variant, in
being a 'negative' deception, because the splendidly attired surrogate
fails to fool the sacred spring and the ruse fails.

4. A Quest

These narratives feature a younger brother who undertakes a journey,
and in Narratives 1 and 2 involves a quest to fulfil an obligation. In
Narratives 3 and 4 the younger brother returns to the material domain
apparently for good, the cycle completed, duty to his social superior
discharged, and freely-given life-sustaining help rendered a deity –
with benefits accruing to himself. In Narrative 1 the youngest brother
goes in search of water and food and returns to his elder brothers after
a failed quest. Nevertheless, he proves to be the agency that enables
human beings to obtain life and abundance: in this case the creation
of their descent group and the rights that it will henceforth possess.

5. An Artefact of Impairment

The motif of the artefact of impairment (a cultural tool) projects the
domain of matter into that of spirit thereby securing the benefits that
result from the exchanges between these two ontological spheres.
Enhanced by the support of the other motifs, this is accomplished
within the natural medium of water, the procreative agency that
makes life, health, and abundance possible.

6. Life, Health, and Abundance

Many Timorese rituals are carried out to obtain life, fertility, and
abundance – essential elements of the human experience – and
sometimes (explicitly and sometimes implicitly) they require ex-

---

not to become dependent and thereby place himself in an inferior status
to a predator.

changes between human beings and spirits. As this set of narratives shows, the same is true for oral literature; to rephrase Roy Rappaport (1999: 161), such narratives provide a medium for speakers and listeners to communicate their connections with the other world and communicate the meaning of existence.

WATER AS AN AGENT OF TRANSFORMATION

The transforming agency of water in these narratives is of great consequence for human beings and spirits alike. It is the medium that provides the link between the material world and the spiritual world, whether the quest, which brings it into play, involves submergence in it or travel across it. In Narrative 4 it becomes a dynamic force, disclosing a deception on the part of the younger brother of serious social consequence; it causes a couple to vanish; and ultimately brings about the destruction of an entire community.

Balthasar Kehi and Lisa Palmer (2012) have described how water is an pervasive or holistic element central to both the expression of cosmological ideas for the Timorese and for the understanding of life itself. This significance is attested to by the fact that Timorese kingdoms in Portuguese times and districts today often have names that link them with water (Palmer 2015: 29).[14] And, as Jorge Duarte (1964: 1) and others have shown, water when employed in ritual bridges the divide between the human realm and the otherwise inaccessible realm of the spirit; and between the material domain and the spiritual domain. On the one hand water distances the human from the 'other', yet, on the other hand, makes possible their mediation and conjunction.

As we have seen, springs in particular function as a threshold for exchange and reciprocity between the visible and invisible worlds. For the Mambai of Aileu: 'At the sacred springs where the central rites unfold, the living reencounter the shades of the dead, who return from the sea' (Traube 1986: 185). Among the Makassai and

---

14 McWilliam (2007) also mentions how many of the Fataluku names for places and settlements refer to water – usually places where one finds it.

Wai Ma'a, sacred springs provide a passage between life and death (Palmer 2015: 75) and are often considered to be the ultimate source of life and death (Kehi & Palmer 2012).

I have argued here that this theme is also reflected in the verbal arts of Timor. In these narratives water furnishes an environment conducive to the two cosmological domains of spirit and matter conjoining to facilitate the exchange of benefits. Although of a material nature, water, because it is the location of spirit, possesses a more ambiguous character than the material world, which is why it functions as an agent of transformation, the most striking of which involve: (a) transformation from matter to spirit and from spirit to matter; (b) transformation from health to sickness and from sickness to health; (c) transformation from inferior to superior and from superior to inferior; and (d) transformation from visible to invisible and from invisible to visible. As an aquatic enabler and natural substance, water is the counterpart of the impaling artefact, an instrument unambiguously emblematic of the material world. Both water and artefact, however, bring about the entrapment of spirit and make possible a fertile interaction between matter and spirit.

In these narratives, denizens of two interdependent ontological domains, disjoined yet conjoined by water, mutually sustain each other in a reciprocal relationship because spirits and human beings rely upon each other for necessities essential for their respective existences. As we saw in Chapter 6, this interdependency was discussed in a contradictory fashion by Marcel Mauss. In his earlier work on the sacrifice with Henri Hubert (Mauss and Hubert 1888) he argued that human beings and their gods were mutually interdependent and that their relationship was not one of hierarchy but of equality. Subsequently, however, in his essay on the gift (Mauss 1950) he proposed that, because the gifts that human beings sacrificed to their gods were much inferior to the prestations that gods gave to their human partners, the human beings were of lower status in the ontological hierarchy that he later detected. Mauss' ambivalence is reflected in these narratives. In Narrative 1 the eel sacrifices himself for his brothers, and Mauss would presumably regard him as moving from a subordinate younger brother to a superordinate creator god. Again, in Narrative 2, the spirit becomes the wife-giving superior of the younger brother, the opposite of what happens in Narrative 4.

One may ask why eels, crocodiles, and fish are used as animal representations of the spiritual domain. One possible explanation is suggested by Palmer (20015: 253, n. 9) who points out that the biological properties and environmental habits of these aquatic creatures evoke the notion of transformation. They are born from eggs laid outside the body and alter their appearance; and they also live on land as well as in water. Another possible explanation might lie in the fact that they are creatures whose principal natural habitat is water, dwellers in a medium that is not only ambiguous but also invisible to the human eye. Living under water they cannot be seen by those who dwell on dry land and thus function as handy symbols of the invisible world.

CONCLUSION

All four narratives considered in this chapter may be of Tetum provenance, but it would be a mistake to suppose that this category of narrative is exclusive to that ethno-linguistic population, for as I discuss elsewhere (Hicks 2016), they also occur in the oral literature of other populations, including populations outside Timor-Leste.[15] Nor should it be supposed that these motifs are exclusive to any particular vernacular typology. They can be conscripted to suit a variety of purposes: status reversal, for example, also occurs in animal fables, such as one narrative in which the mentally challenged shark outwits the clever monkey (Hicks 1984) or Narrative 1 in Chapter 2 in which Dog triumphs over Monkey. But the narratives discussed here would appear to form a discrete category of narrative insofar as the motifs are combined within the confines of a given tale. In the Timorese vernacular, or 'emic', indigenous classification narratives are distin-

---

15 They include the Meto, Bunak, Makassai, and Nauete, and certain populations in the Alor Peninsula and on Sumbawa.

guished as 'legends' (Tetum: *lian tuan*), 'myths,' 'folktales,' 'fables,' 'morality tales,' or 'just-so stories' (Tetum: a*iknananoik*).[16]

In the present chapter we have seen how these motifs combine consistently and repetitively in such a manner as to produce narratives that justify their being regarded as a category of narrative distinct from this indigenous classification, an etic category of narrative, derived from an outsider's perspective, one that provides us with an alternative perspective upon what Father Ezequiel Enes Pascoal (1967) has called '*A Alma de Timor vista na sua Fantasia*' – 'The Timorese soul seen in its imagination'. An imagination which makes water the (tangible) means of what brings about exchange and facilitates conjunction between spirit and matter.

REFERENCES

Barnes, Susana 2011. 'Origins, Precedence and Social Order in the Domain of Ina Ama Beli Darlari'. In *Land and Life in Timor-Leste. Ethnographic Essays,* Andrew McWilliam and Elizabeth Traube (eds). Canberra, ANU E-press pp. 23–46.

—— 2017. 'The Re-assertion of Sacralized Authority in Post-Occupation Uato-Lari'. In *Transformations in Independent Timor-Leste: Dynamics of Social and Cultural Cohabitations,* edited by Susana de Matos Viegas and Rui Graça Feijó. Routledge: Taylor and Francis Group: London and New York.

Bovensiepen, Judith M. 2011. 'Opening and Closing the Land: Land and power in the Idaté highlands'. In Andrew McWilliam and Elizabeth Traube (eds). *Land and Life in Timor-Leste. Ethnographic Essays*: 47–60.

Duarte, Jorge Barros n.d. *A Nascente 'Lulic' de Corlúli*. Unpublished MS.

—— 1964. 'Barlaque', in *Seara* (n.s.) 2 (3–4): 92–119. *Suplemento Boletim Eclesiástico da Diocese de Dili, Timor Português*. (Repub-

---

16 I am grateful to Dr Elizabeth Traube for noting that these six motifs cross narrational genres, some being 'practical', i.e., of political importance and economic significance, others being 'fanciful'.

lished with emendations as 'Barlaque: casamento gentílico timo-rense'. *Arquivos Centro Cultural Português*, XIV: 377– 418 (1979).

—— 1984. *Timor: Ritos e Mitos Ataúros*. Lisbon: Instituto Cultura e Língua Portuguesa, Ministério da Educação, Divisão de Publicações.

Forth, Gregory 1998. *Beneath the Volcano: religion, cosmology and spir-it classification among the Nage of eastern Indonesia. Verhandelingen van het Koninklijk Instituut voor Taal-, Land- en Volkenkunde 177*. Leiden: KITLV Press.

Hicks, David 1974. 'The Tetum Folktale as a Sociological, Cosmo-logical, and Logical Model' in *Anthropos* 69: 57–67. Republished in 1978 in David Hicks, *Structural Analysis in Anthropology: Case Studies from Indonesia and Brazil*. St. Augustin: Anthropos Insti-tut, Pp. 63–71.

—— 1984. *A Maternal Religion: the role of women in Tetum myth and ritu-al*. DeKalb: Northern Illinois University, Center for Southeast Asian Studies. Monograph Series on Southeast Asia. Special Report No. 22.

—— 1988. 'Literary Masks and Metaphysical Truths: intimations from Timor', in *American Anthropologist* 90 (4): 807–817.

—— 1996. 'Making the King Divine: a case study in ritual regicide from Timor' in *Journal of the Royal Anthropological Institute* 2 (4): 611–624.

—— 1998 'Divine Kings and Younger Brothers on Timor'. In Lorraine V. Aragon and Susan Russell (eds), *Structuralism's Transformations: Order and Revisions in Indonesian and Malaysian Societies*. Tempe, Arizona State University: 35–47.

—— 2007 'Younger Brother and Fishing Hook on Timor: reas-sessing Mauss on hierarchy and divinity' in *Journal of the Royal Anthropological Institute (new series)* 13 (1): 39–56.

Hubert, Henri & Marcel Mauss 1888. 'Essai sur la nature et la fonc-tion du sacrifice'. *L'Année Sociologique* 2, 29–238.

Kehi, Balthasar & Lisa Palmer 2012. 'Hamatak Halirin: The cosmo-logical and socio-ecological roles of water in Koba Lima, Timor', in *Bijdragen tot de Taal-, Land- en Volkenkunde*, 168: 445–471.

Lévi-Strauss, Claude 1979. *Myth and Meaning: cracking the code of culture*. New York, Shocken Books.

Mauss, Marcel 1950. '*Essai sur le don: forme et raison de l'échange dans les sociétés archaïques*' in Marcel Mauss (ed) *Sociologie et anthropologie*. Paris, Presses Universitaires de France: 143–279.

Middlekoop, P. 1958. 'Four tales with mythical features characteristic of the Timorese people', in *Bijdragen toot de Taal-, Land- en Volkenkunde* 114: 384–405.

Palmer, Lisa 2015. *Water Politics and Spiritual Ecology: Custom, governance and development*. London and New York: Routledge.

Pascoal, Ezequiel Enes 1967. *A Alma de Timor Vista Na Sua Fantasia: lendas, fábula e contos*. Braga: Barbosa & Xavier, Lda.

Rappaport, Roy. 1999. *Ritual and Religion in the Making of Humanity*, Cambridge: Cambridge University Press.

Rodemeier, Susanne. 2009. 'Bui Hangi – the Deity's Human Wife'. *Anthropos* 104: 469–482.

Sá, Artur Basílio de 1961. *Textos em Teto Literatura Oral Timorense*, *Vol. 1*. Lisboa, Junta de Investigações do Ultramar, Estudos de Ciências Politicas e Sociais 45.

Sousa, Lúcio Manuel Gomes de. 2015. Personal communication.

Traube, Elizabeth 1987. *Cosmology and Social Life*. Chicago: University of Chicago Press.

Epilogue

For the anthropologist, Bronislaw Malinowski, the genre of narrative that we call 'myths' serves social functions. The narratives justify custom or give those who chose to manipulate their themes political ammunition for asserting authority or contesting land-claims. They are moreover, he argued, specimens of performative art. Some tales in this volume tend to support this claim at the same time as they give us a sense of the many faces that oral narrative can present, and so invite attention by the historian, psychologist, and folklorist as well as providing ethnographic material for an analytical perspective. I hope to have demonstrated that the plots and characters depicted here in narrative form may be understood as allegories that convey metaphysical ideas. These essays reveal the explanatory potentials of an intellectual approach in enabling us to find deeper meaning in apparently trivial tales, a meaning that perhaps merits the term 'metaphysical resonance'.

Thus, while some tales might at first hearing (or reading) seem to offer escapist adventures, grotesque characters, and implausible outcomes suitable only for entertainment, for listeners and readers inclined to consider the possibility that they may hide deeper meanings than they apparently offer, I hope to have shown a source of thought-provoking stimulations to challenge the intellect. They invite questions.

One question, for example, was posed and answered in Chapter 8 by Lisa Palmer. Why do crocodiles and eels so ubiquitously represent human beings or are endowed with certain humanlike traits? She finds, as we saw, a cogent answer in their biological quality of transformation, a Timorese example of how an indigenous population uses its observation of the biological properties of natural species in its oral narratives to express significant ideas, an observation made by Lévi-Strauss in the context of Amerindian mythology.

Another question – one having more expansive application – is why do these narratives so often make use of the animal kingdom for many of their characters? Scholars sharing with Malinowski a proclivity for explaining customary thought and behaviour in pragmatic terms might find that the answer lies in Radcliffe-Brown's explanation for animal symbols employed in totemic representations: because 'animals are goods to eat' (*bonnes à manger*).[1] Lévi-Strauss, on the other hand, suggests an intellectual reason – because 'animals are goods to think [with]' (*bonnes à pense*) (Leach 1970: 34). In these narratives the spirit-animals that inhabit the wet underworld contrast with human beings who inhabit the dry upperworld, whose prime representative is the elder brother who initially commands precedence over the younger brother. From a Lévi-Straussian perspective the relationship between the two domains and their inhabitants is one of *disjunction* (or *separation*). The younger brother's status is different. The subordinate brother transcends both worlds, moving between them with disregard for the disjunction symbolized by the elder brother in a manner that implies a relationship of *conjunction* (or *contiguity*). These two types of relationship form components of a metaphysical construction of reality that I have elsewhere posited for the Tetum-speakers of Viqueque as one of 'conjunction-leading-to-creation' and 'disjunction-leading-to-re-creation' (Hicks 1973; 1985).

REFERENCES

Hicks, David 1973 *An Ethnographic Study of a Timorese People*. DPhil. dissertation, University of Oxford.

———1985. '*Conjonction féminine et disjunction masculine chez les Tetum*' (*Timor, Indonésie Oriental*). *L'Homme* 25 (2): 23–36.

Leach, Edmund 1970. *Claude Lévi-Strauss*. London: Fontana/Collins.

---

1 I doubt if Radcliffe-Brown had crocodiles in mind, though!

Index

abundance 47, 67, 89, 93, 101, 106, 120, 128, 136, 138, 150, 159, 160, 171, 173. *See also* plenitude

adat xiii, 1, 5. *See also* custom; *lisan*

affine 27, 34, 39, 48, 57. *See also* kinship

affinity 9, 41, 159, 165, 167

agnation 159, 165, 167

ahi matan xiii, 10, 91. *See also* descent groups; source

aiknananoik xiii, 3, 107, 177

alliance xiv, 4, 36, 37, 38, 39, 40, 41, 42, 45, 50, 51, 57, 59, 60, 61, 101, 105, 132, 138, 171

alliance group 37, 41, 42

alternation 132, 146, 159, 171

alin-feto xiii

alin-mane xiii, 1, 12. *See also* younger brother

Alor xvii, 131, 136, 176

ancestor xiv, 1, 5, 13, 14, 15, 16, 18, 19, 26, 27, 28, 44, 47, 48, 67, 102, 107, 108, 124, 132, 161, 163, 164. *See also mate bein*

arrow 84, 115, 116, 128, 136, 143, 159. *See also* artefact

artefact ix, 1, 16, 17, 18, 19, 27, 28, 44, 83, 100, 103, 106, 109, 110, 118, 119, 120, 121, 124, 129, 131, 143, 150, 159, 160, 163, 165, 173, 175. *See also* arrow; heirloom; hook; machete

asymmetric alliance xiv, 36, 37, 57, 59, 61, 132, 138

Atabae 56, 57, 59, 64, 66, 67, 77, 78, 87, 89, 167

Atoni 6, 29, 49, 77, 93, 118, 137. *See also* language; Meto

Balibo 56, 57, 59, 63, 64, 66, 67, 77, 78, 83, 89

bard. *See lia na'in*; teller of tales

barlaki xiii, 10, 47. *See also barlaque*

barlaque vii, xii, xiii, 1, 10, 28, 31, 32, 33, 35, 37, 39, 40, 41, 42, 43, 45, 46, 47, 48, 49, 50, 51, 73, 177, 178. *See also barlaki*

Baucau xvii, 33, 143, 155, 163

Barnes, R. H. 93

Barnes, Susana 159, 163, 177

belak xiii, 15, 16, 18. *See also* heirloom

Bemalai ix, 16, 55, 56, 57, 58, 59

berlaki. See barlaki; barlaque

Bima 129, 131, 134, 135, 136, 155

Bimanese 132

boundary 15, 40, 66, 67, 131, 143, 153

Bovensiepen, Judith 3, 4, 15, 16, 17, 28, 65, 68, 160, 177

boar 136, 151

buffalo xiv, 7, 11, 13, 14, 19, 38, 43, 57, 61, 65, 66, 81, 82, 83, 85, 86, 89, 90, 113, 114, 115, 128, 132,

NIAS – Nordic Institute of Asian Studies
New and Recent Monographs

NIAS Press is the autonomous publishing arm of NIAS – Nordic Institute of Asian Studies, a research institute located at the University of Copenhagen. NIAS is partially funded by the governments of Denmark, Finland, Iceland, Norway and Sweden via the Nordic Council of Ministers, and works to encourage and support Asian studies in the Nordic countries. In so doing, NIAS has been publishing books since 1969, with more than two hundred titles produced in the past few years.

UNIVERSITY OF COPENHAGEN

norden
Nordic Council of Ministers

Printed by Printforce, United Kingdom